Our Seamen

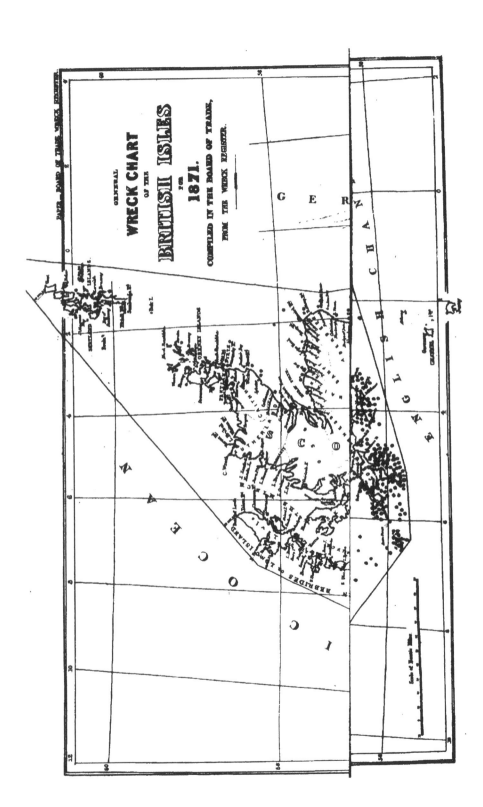

GENERAL
WRECK CHART
OF THE
BRITISH ISLES.
FOR
1871.
COMPILED IN THE BOARD OF TRADE,
FROM THE WRECK REGISTER.

OUR SEAMEN.

AN APPEAL.

BY

SAMUEL PLIMSOLL, M.P.

POPULAR EDITION.

LONDON:

VIRTUE & CO., 26, IVY LANE,

PATERNOSTER ROW.

1873.

LONDON :

PRINTED BY VIRTUE AND CO.,

CITY ROAD.

PREFACE.

EVERYBODY knows that there is a great loss of life on our coasts annually, and nearly everybody deplores it. I am sure that if the English public equally knew how much of this loss is preventible, and the means of preventing it, no long time would elapse before means would be taken to secure this end.

It is with the view of giving this information, so as to enable each person who reads these pages to pronounce with decision upon this question, that this pamphlet is submitted to the public.

I have kept steadily in mind the idea of writing to an individual, as otherwise I should not have had the courage to address the public in what (from its length alone) looks like a book. As to a portion of it, I (perhaps naturally) shrink a good deal from submitting it to the public. It seemed, however, in writing it, and still seems to me, to give weight to my testimony on behalf of the working men. I apologise to any of my friends who may feel annoyed, and who would doubtless have aided me had they known of the straits to which I was brought in the earlier part of my life in London; but I ask them to think what a grand and glorious thing it will be if, by *any* sacrifice, we can put a stop to the dreadful and the shameful waste of precious human life which is now going on.

I thank all those gentlemen in the east, in the west, in the north, in the south, and in London, who have so greatly assisted me for some years in my inquiries, but they would not thank me if I thanked them by name. They are, however, one and all, longing to tell a Royal Commission all they have told to me—and more; for then they would speak under the protection of the law, whereas now they have to depend upon my discretion.

I intended to treat the subject at greater length, describing surveys for continuation, restoration, and some other matters, but, fearing to make my Appeal too long—when nobody would read it—I have curtailed it.

NOTE TO THE PRESENT EDITION.

THIS Edition has been prepared in answer to requests that have reached me from many parts of the country. It only remains for me gratefully to acknowledge the generous reception that has been accorded to my Appeal, and to record my confident belief that a man's greatest safeguard is publicity, so long as his purpose, and the means he uses to attain it, are single.

As the note upon the first page indicates, in the Large Edition of this Appeal I reproduced in fac-simile, by means of photography, the various letters, official documents, &c., used in support of my argument. In this Edition all that is essential has been very carefully copied, and appears in smaller type. This will explain any occasional appearance of abruptness in the beginning or ending of a quotation: for instance, on page 2 the passage quoted forms two pages of a magazine; the *list* referred to in the first line appeared on a previous page of that magazine.

SAMUEL PLIMSOLL.

CONTENTS.

————•————

OUR SEAMEN.

I HAVE no idea of writing a book.   I don't know how
to do`it, and fear I could not succeed if I tried; the
idea, therefore, is very formidable to me.

I will suppose myself to be writing to an individual, and
to be saying all I could think of to induce him to lend his
utmost aid in remedying the great evil which we all deplore;
and I will write, so far as I can, just as I would speak to
him if he were now sitting by my side. If he were so sitting,
there are sundry papers I should like to show him in con-
firmation of my statements and opinions, so that he might
know for himself how absolutely true they are.

I cannot quite do this in your case, but very nearly ; I can
have them photographed,* and then you will see them as
really and truly as if they were held to a glass and you were
looking at their reflection in it.

Now, there are many hundreds of lives lost annually by
shipwreck, and as to the far greater part of them, they are
lost from causes which are easily preventible.   I may say
further, that they would not be lost if the same care was
taken of our sailors by the law as is taken of the rest of our

---

* In the quarto edition of this book every piece of evidence was
photographed from the original documents.   In this cheaper edition
these are given in smaller type, after a word-for-word comparison.

B

fellow-subjects. A great number of ships are regularly sent to sea in such a rotten and otherwise ill-provided state that they *can* only reach their destination through fine weather, and a large number are so overloaded that it is nearly impossible for them also to reach their destination if the voyage is at all rough. And I can show you that from these two causes alone (and they apply only to one portion of our merchant ships) rather more than a full half of our losses arise.

As to the first of these statements, it would need no support if you lived in a seaport town, for you would then know it from observation and common conversation; but I suppose you to be an inhabitant of one of our large inland towns (it being far more important to convince this population than that of the others, for reformation can only begin when our people inland are well informed on this subject).

The statements in the following quotation are taken from " The Life-Boat " for Nov. 1, 1870, the journal of the Committee of the National Life-Boat Institution, a body having ample information and knowledge, and not likely to make any statement without careful consideration (the italics are my own) :—

[A noticeable feature of this list is, that ships comparatively new are lost in greater proportion than those which are old. Thus we find that up to fourteen years 1,130 were lost, and from fifteen to thirty there were 750, while there were 341 old ships between thirty and fifty, and 87 very old ships, one of which was 94, and another nearly a hundred years old ! The last-named vessel was a collier, and it had seven persons on board when it was wrecked, one of whom only was saved.

We have repeatedly, through the medium of this Journal, strongly called attention to the terribly rotten state of many of the ships above twenty years old ; in too many instances, on such vessels getting ashore, their crews perish before there is any possibility of getting out the life-boat from the shore to their help.

From a Table giving the localities of the wrecks, we have compiled, on an admirable plan suggested by HENRY JEULA, Esq., the Honorary Secretary of the Statistical Committee of Lloyd's, the following particulars, giving the average percentage of the disasters according to the different parts of the coasts of the United Kingdom on which they happened :—

Parts of the Coasts.	Percentage.
EAST COAST: Dungeness to Duncansby Head (inclusive) .	56·30
WEST COAST: Land's End to Mull of Cantyre (inclusive) .	23·41
SOUTH COAST: Dungeness to Land's End (exclusive) . .	10·08
IRISH COAST	7·00
North and West Coasts of Scotland, from the Mull of Cantyre to Duncansby Head; including the Northern Islands, Hebrides, Islay, Orkney, Shetland, &c.	1·84
Isle of Man, Scilly Islands, and Lundy Island - . .	1·37
	100·

As usual, the largest number of wrecks occurred on the east coast, although the loss of life was not greatest there. The largest loss of life, during the ten years ending in 1869, was in the Irish Sea and on its coasts.

Owing to the admirable and detailed manner in which the *Register* is worked out, we are enabled to denote the mode in which the different wrecks were rigged. Thus we find that of those which happened in 1869, 98 were fitted as ships, 192 were steam vessels, 706 schooners, 468 brigs, 327 barques, 265 brigantines, and 178 smacks, the remainder being mostly smaller craft, rigged in various ways. Schooners and brigs, as usual, furnish the greatest number of wrecks, that being the ordinary class of rig of our coasting vessels.

The Table which distinguishes the wrecks in 1869, according to the force of the wind when they happened, is a highly instructive one. It is as follows :—

Force of Wind.	Vessels.
Calm	19
Light air. Just sufficient to give steerage way . . .	28
Light breeze ⎫ With which a ship with all ⎧ 1 to 2 knots	100
Gentle breeze ⎬ sail set and clean full, would ⎨ 3 to 4 knots	30
Moderate breeze ⎭ go in smooth water . . ⎩ 5 to 6 knots	178
Fresh breeze ⎫ In which she ⎧ Royals, &c.	220
Strong breeze ⎪ could just ⎪ Single reefs and T. G. sails	262
Moderate gale ⎬ ⎨ Double reefs and jib . .	77
Fresh gale ⎪ carry ⎪ Triple reefs, &c. . .	63
Strong gale ⎭ going free ⎩ Close reefs and courses .	700
Whole gale, in which she could just bear close-reefed main-topsail and reefed foresail	157
Storm. Under storm staysail	39
Hurricane. Under bare poles	141
Unknown	100
Total . . .	2,114

This reveals the remarkable fact that no less than 177 wrecks happened when the wind was either perfectly calm, or at most there was not more than a gentle breeze 'blowing, and that 660 vessels were lost in moderate, fresh, and strong breezes.

We notice that of the 606 total wrecks during the past year on our shores, not counting collisions, 74 arose from defects in the ships or their equipments, such as imperfect charts, compasses, &c.—45 of them, indeed, being caused by absolute unseaworthiness; 80 occurred through the fault of those on board; 71 parted their cables or dragged their anchors, and went on shore; 57 were lost from the damage to hull or the loss of masts, yards, or sails; 119 foundered; 3 capsized; and the rest were wrecked in various other ways.

It is a lamentable fact that, irrespective of collisions, 154 vessels should thus have been totally lost in one year—we fear, in too many instances through the shortcomings of man, attended, as these disasters too frequently were, with a deplorable loss of life.

And, as regards those casualties, 1,047 in number, classed as "partial losses other than collisions," it appears that 156 of them were caused by carelessness, and 72 by defects in the ships or their gear; and, taking the record of the past ten years, we grieve to say that 3,249 vessels were either totally or partially lost from such really preventible causes in that period; and the loss of life in such cases must, of course, have been truly alarming.

We moreover find that 571 vessels were wrecked last year that were under the command of masters who held certificates of competency; and that in 264 cases the masters held certificates of service; while the large number of 1,135 were lost which were under the command of persons who were not legally compelled—as most assuredly they should have been—to possess such certificates of competency, besides 389 that had foreign masters not holding British certificates. In 235 cases it is not known whether or not the masters held certificates.

On analysing the tonnage of the vessels lost last year, it proves to be as follows :—

	Vessels.
Vessels under 50 Tons	462
51 and under 100 ,, ...	616
101 ,, 300 ,, ...	996
301 ,, 600 ,, ...	371
601 ,, 900 ,, ...	73
901 ,, 1200 ,, ...	49
1200 and upwards ,, ...	25
Unknown	2
Total . . .	2,594

As respects cargoes, it seems that 691 were laden colliers, 183 colliers in ballast, 139 vessels having metallic ore on board, 187 with stone ores, &c., 153 were fishing-smacks, and 1,241 were ships with other cargoes or in ballast.

As usual, the ships of the collier class employed in the regular carrying trade have suffered severely; they numbered 1,200, or about half the whole body of ships to which accidents happened during the year. Thus it is, in a great measure, that so many casualties occur on our coasts, *for such is the notoriously ill-found and unseaworthy man-ner in which these vessels are sent on their voyages, that in every gale—even if it be one of a moderate character only—it becomes a certainty that numbers of them will be destroyed, as will be seen from the fact that* 844 *of them were lost in* 1864; 935 *in* 1865; 1,150 *in* 1866; 1,215 *in* 1867; 1,014 *in* 1868; *and* 1,200 *in* 1869—*or* 6,357 *in six years.*

It is overwhelming to contemplate the loss of life from these, in too many instances, avoidable wrecks.

Turning now to the cases of collisions at sea off our coasts, which are often of a very distressing character, the number reported last year, as we have before observed, is 461 ; and of these 148 occurred in the day-time, and 313 at night. The numbers given for the year 1868 were 99 in the day and 280 in the night. Those for 1869, again, give 90 as total and 371 as partial wrecks ; and of the total wrecks no less than 29 happened from bad look-out, 16 from want of proper observance of the steering and sailing rules, 8 from thick and foggy weather, and 37 from other causes.

Of the partial losses through collision, 66 were from bad look-out, 53 were from neglect or misapplication of steering and sailing rules, 23 from want of seamanship, 33 from general negligence and want of caution, 11 from neglecting to show proper light, and 185 from various other causes.

The nature of the collisions is thus described :—17 occurred between steamers, and 193 between sailing-vessels while both were under way ; 76 collisions also happened between sailing-vessels, one being at anchor and the other under way ; 66 between steamers and sailing-vessels, both being under way ; and only 13 were caused by steamers running into sailing-vessels at anchor ; 4 by sailing-vessels under way running into steamers at anchor ; and none by one steamer coming into collision with another at anchor ; 92 collisions also occurred through vessels breaking from their anchors or moorings.]

The next statement is made by no less an authority than the Government itself, for the Tables on pp. 6—11 are part of the Annual Report of the Board of Trade, and I beg your attention to the words which I have printed in italics :—

[Of the 841 casualties,—*i.e.*, partial losses from causes other than collisions,—487 happened when the wind was at force 9 or upwards (a strong gale), and are included as having been caused by stress of weather ; 123 arose from carelessness ; 82 from defects in the ship or her equipments ; and the remainder appear to have arisen from various other causes.

This is shown in the following short Table :—

	Wrecks resulting in Total Loss.					Casualties resulting in Partial Damage.					
Year.	Arising from Stress of Weather.	Arising from In-attention, Careless-ness, and Neglect.	Arising from Defects in Ships or Equip-ments.	Arising from various Causes.	Arising from Causes unknown.	Arising from Stress of Weather.	Arising from In-attention, Careless-ness, and Neglect.	Arising from Defects in Ships or Equip-ments.	Arising from various Causes.	Arising from Causes unknown.	Total.
1859	298	84	42	70	33	308	97	42	88	5	1,067
1860	278	103	49	40	6	367	110	49	72	7	1,081
1861	302	89	48	49	25	424	102	56	75	1	1,171
1862	242	72	25	96	20	386	115	42	144	8	1,150
1863	332	61	31	65	14	550	115	30	126	9	1,333
1864	163	89	39	64	31	299	148	53	144	9	1,039
1865	245	99	38	61	27	501	137	48	129	17	1,302
1866	276	125	74	68	19	529	119	44	174	10	1,438
1867	385	106	65	84	16	653	138	85	135	9	1,676
1868	265	87	71	85	19	487	123	82	143	6	1,368
Total for 10 Years	2,786	1,397		892		4,504	1,735		1,311		12,625

The total number of ships which, according to the facts reported, appear to have foundered or to have been otherwise totally lost on our coasts from unseaworthiness, unsound gear, &c. (Class 3), in the last ten years, is 482; and the number of casualties arising from the same causes, during the same period, and resulting in partial damage, is 531.

In 1868 there were 131 wrecks and casualties to smacks and other fishing-vessels. Excluding these 131 fishing-vessels, it will be seen that the number of vessels employed in the regular carrying trade that have suffered from wreck or casualty during the year is 2,000. If this number is again subdivided it will be found that *about half of it is represented by the unseaworthy, overladen, or ill-found vessels of the collier class chiefly employed in the coasting trade. For the six years ending* 1868 *the number is more than half. This will be more readily apparent by the following short Table :—*

Ships.	1863. No.	1864. No.	1865. No.	1866. No.	1867. No.	1868. No.
Fishing smacks	132	74	98	116	188	131
Colliers laden	614	523	535	726	713	640
Colliers in ballast	114	99	140	129	242	100
Metallic ores	146	126	150	141	110	127
Stone ores	115	96	109	154	150	147
(bracketed total)	989	844	934	1,150	1,215	1,014 !
Ships with other cargoes, and other ships in ballast	880	823	980	1,023	1,110	986 !
Total ships	2,001	1,741	2,012	2,289	2,513	2,131

From Table 4 it will be seen that in the ten years ended 1868 disasters to comparatively new ships bear a very high proportion to the whole number; that 176 wrecks and casualties happened to nearly new ships, and 297 to ships from three to seven years of age. Then there are wrecks and casualties to 420 ships from seven to 14 years old, and to 653 from 15 to 30 years old. Then follow 267 old ships from 30 to 50 years old. Having passed the service of half a century we come to the very old ships, viz., 35 between 50 and 60 years old, 28 from 60 to 70, 9 from 70 to 80. . . . .   ]

[The total number of ships which, according to the facts reported, appear to have foundered or to have been otherwise totally lost on and near the coasts of the United Kingdom from unseaworthiness, unsound gear, &c. (Class 3 of preceding Table), in the last ten years, is 524; and the number of casualties arising from the same causes, during the same period, and resulting in partial damage, is 655.

In 1871, there were on and near the coasts of the United Kingdom 120 wrecks and casualties to smacks and other fishing-vessels. Excluding these 120 fishing-vessels, *it will be seen that the number of vessels employed in the regular carrying trade that have suffered from wreck or casualty here during the year is* 1,807. *If this number is again subdivided it will be found that nearly half of it is represented by vessels of the collier class, chiefly employed in the coasting trade. For the seven years ending* 1871 *the number is more than half.* This will be more readily seen from the Table on following page (page 9).

From Table 4 in the Abstract it will be seen that in the ten years ended 1871, disasters on and near the coasts of the United Kingdom to comparatively new ships bear a very high proportion to the whole number; and that during the year 1871, 155 wrecks and casualties happened to nearly new ships, and 302 to ships from three to seven years of age. Then there are wrecks and casualties to 361 ships from seven to 14 years old, and to 554 from 15 to 30 years old. Then follow 265 old ships from 30 to 50 years old. Having passed the service of half a century we come to the very old ships, viz., 44 between 50 and 60 years old, 19 from 60 to 70, 6 from 70 to 80, 8 from 80 to 90, and 3 upwards of 100. The ages of 210 are unknown.

Of the 1,927 vessels lost or damaged on and near the coasts of the United Kingdom in 1871, 84 were rigged as ships, 223 were steamships, 493 schooners, 282 brigs, 232 barques, 219 brigantines, and 103 smacks; the remainder were small vessels rigged in various ways. Of the 1,927 vessels referred to, 806 did not exceed 100 tons burden; 687 were from 100 to 300 tons, 279 were from 300 to 600 tons, and 155 only were above 600 tons burden.

From Table 8, showing the parts of the coasts on which the wrecks and casualties on and near the coasts of the United Kingdom happened, it will be seen that, as usual, the greatest number occurred on the East coast. The numbers are as follow :—

East Coast	793
South Coast	201
West Coast	397
N. and W. Coast of Ireland	32

Ships.	1865. No.	1866. No.	1867. No.	1868. No.	1869. No.	1870. No.	1871. No.
Fishing smacks . . .	98	116	188	131	153	83	120
Colliers laden .	535	726	713	640	691	491	506
Colliers in ballast	140 } 934*	129 } 1,150*	242 } 1,215⁴	100 } 1,014*	183 } 1,200*	88 } 820*	115 } 898*
Metallic ores .	150	141	110	127	139	126	160
Stone ores . .	109	154	150	147	187	115	117
Ships with other cargoes, and other ships in ballast † .	200	1,023	1,110	986	1,241	962	909
Total ships . .	2,012	2,219	2,513	2,131	2,594	1,865	1,927

(* All these preventible. This does not include over-sea voyages.—S.P.)

Irish Coast 125
Isle of Man 12
Lundy Island 5
Scilly Isles 10

The winds appear from the wreck reports to have been destructive to shipping on and near the coasts of the United Kingdom during the ten years ended 1871, in the proportions following :—

Direction.	WRECKS, ETC., IN										Total.
	1862.	1863.	1864.	1865.	1866.	1867.	1868.	1869.	1870.	1871.	
N.. .	65	46	19	61	37	136	53	109	53	45	624
N.N.E.	45	31	26	59	38	116	46	114	37	50	562
N.E. .	51	30	56	90	97	153	88	161	60	71	857
E.N.E.	44	29	44	58	92	75	56	74	57	61	590
E.. .	29	26	81	55	69	83	61	57	96	70	627
E.S.E. .	45	27	92	56	41	107	35	41	42	89	575
S.E. .	61	50	97	97	90	164	64	53	88	111	873
S.S.E. .	43	36	83	60	69	84	56	48	54	86	619
S.. .	61	47	61	94	129	61	74	113	84	102	826
S.S.W.	139	76	95	133	157	93	160	126	77	124	1,180
S.W. .	194	159	142	192	206	181	223	221	145	169	1,832
W.S.W.	140	147	81	102	174	102	144	135	92	95	1,212
W. .	89	137	92	73	105	103	120	116	113	75	1,023
W.N.W.	75	209	77	91	101	92	108	134	81	69	1,037
N.W. .	110	214	70	101	115	126	116	149	83	79	1,163
N.N.W.	62	94	21	59	45	80	55	131	31	23	601
	1,253	1,358	1,137	1,381	1,565	1,756	1,459	1,782	1,193	1,319	14,203

(Grouped totals: 624; {562, 857, 590, 627, 575, 873, 619} = 4,705; 826; {1,180, 1,832, 1,212, 1,023, 1,037, 1,163, 601} = 8,048)

The above Table shows that westerly winds are far more destructive than easterly winds,—the most destructive being from south-west. It should, however, be remembered that westerly winds are far more common than easterly winds.

It will be seen from Table 10, distinguishing the wrecks, &c., on and near the coasts of the United Kingdom according to the force of the wind at the time at which they happened, that in 1871, 856* *happened when the wind was at force 6 or under, that is to say, when the force of the wind did not exceed a strong breeze, in which the ship could carry single reefs and topgallant sails; that 149 happened with the wind at forces 7 or 8, or a moderate to fresh gale, when a ship, if properly found, manned, and navigated, can keep the sea with safety;* and that 528 happened with the wind at force 9 and upwards, that is to say, from a strong gale to a hurricane. In other words, 856 happened when the wind was such that a ship could carry her topgallant sails; 149 when a ship ought to be well able to hold her course; and 528 with the wind at and above a strong gale.

The numbers for the last ten years are shown in the following Table :—

---

* Look at this.—S. P.

Force of Wind.	1862.	1863.	1864.	1865.	1866.	1867.	1868.	1869.	1870.	1871.	Total.	
0	23	15	21	20	19	12	17	19	32	32	210	Calm.
1	28	28	19	22	26	26	21	28	48	54	300	Light air. Just sufficient to give steerage way.
2	56	39	97	100	73	63	75	100	129	108	840	Light breeze.
3	43	27	36	24	23	28	33	30	46	55	345	Gentle breeze. (With which a ship with all sail set and clean full would go in smooth water 1 to 2 knots)
4	110	100	142	146	170	160	142	178	153	192	1,493	Moderate breeze. (3 to 4 ,, 5 to 6 ,,)
5	187	174	220	203	225	223	177	220	169	205	2,003	Fresh breeze. (Royals, &c.)
6	195	174	185	163	197	217	196	262	218	210	2,017	Strong breeze. Single reefs and T.G. sails. (In which she could just carry in chase full)
7	75	57	35	47	62	66	75	77	57	79	630	Moderate gale. Double reefs and jib, &c.
8	170	195	39	69	60	105	79	63	84	70	934	Fresh gale. Triple reefs, &c. (and by)
9	199	269	221	552	683	603	534	700	259	314	4,334	Strong gale. Close reefs and courses.
10	218	224	221	120	130	364	195	157	160	167	1,956	Whole gale. (In which she could just bear close-reefed main topsail and reefed foresail.)
11	63	82	30	39	21	52	53	39	25	24	428	Storm. Under storm staysail.
12	69	205	42	99	120	80	53	141	48	23	880	Hurricane. Bare poles.
Var.	6	1	9	2	1	2	—	—	3	9	33	Variable.
Unk.	46	74	73	50	50	89	97	100	71	33	683	Unknown.
	1,488	1,664	1,390	1,656	1,8 0	2,090	1,747	2,114	1,502	1,575	17,086	

Underwriters.—Perhaps you may say (as many besides have said), "But are not nearly all these ships, and their cargoes too, insured? and is it to be supposed that the In-surance Companies" (if you lived in a seaport you would probably say "underwriters," but the general notion is as you put it)—"is it to be supposed that the Insurance people would not see to it, if they were thus plundered; and may we not safely rely upon their self-interest to rectify any wrong-doing in this respect?"

Nor would you be alone in thinking something like this, for a gentleman high in office and in influence at the Board of Trade is reported, in the *Journal of the Society of Arts*, to have said in one of their meetings, "Let ships be lost, and let cargoes be lost, so long as underwriters are too sordid or too lazy to refuse payment of doubtful and fraudulent cases."

Now, as this gentleman, had he been better informed, could long ago have influenced his chiefs to have legis-lated effectively in remedy of the existing state of things, and as there is too much reason to fear that a similar feeling has possessed the public, with the effect of stifling any reviving sense of duty in the matter, you will agree with me that it is of the utmost consequence to spare no pains (if it is a mistake) to show how it is so. The idea is that if a ship has been culpably and shamefully overloaded, or if a ship utterly unfit to go to sea has been sent out to sea insured for as much money as would build a new one, and so bring a positive gain to her owner by her being wrecked, that the Insurance people ought to prove this, and, if they did not bring the guilty to punishment, at least prevent them from making a profit by their wrong-doing.

Now, I want to convince you that this idea is utterly erroneous, and that it would be more reasonable to expect the first person you meet, whether merchant, manufacturer, clergyman, banker, or shopkeeper, to institute inquiry into a fatally fraudulent case of this nature, than to ask the underwriter; because *they* could act without incurring odious mis-representation or loss of business, whilst *these* could only do so at the cost of great suspicion and total loss of future business.

The underwriters cannot move in the matter,—first, *because the loss to each individual underwriter is too small to make it worth his time and trouble.* The popular inland idea of insurance is, that of an individual insuring himself against loss by insuring his house, warehouse, or factory from fire with an insurance company: in the event of the property being destroyed by fire, the company have to pay to him the amount insured by them. They are strong enough to pro-tect themselves, if the insurer has violated the terms of his policy by carelessly exposing the property to unfair risk of fire, or in the rare case of his having purposely fired it; but the circumstances are entirely different in insuring a ship or a cargo. In the latter case, the owner of a ship or freight who wishes to insure applies to an insurance broker, with whom terms are arranged, but only provisionally; the broker informs him on what terms of premium the under-writers are likely to take the risk. If they agree as to what terms will be accepted by the owner or freighter, in the event of the broker succeeding in placing the risk on those terms, the broker then writes out a slip like this—

[B. M. & Co.   9 *Sept.* 1869.

                                                         & Co.

Cash Account.

£5,500 on Hull and Machinery, avge. value £15,000.

SUNSHINE (S.S.)

Clyde   Hong-Kong
           70s.   and 30 days.
Including trial trip and adjusting compasses at Gareloch.

[Here follow Signatures of Underwriters.]

⚓ 1. 600 tons. To sail about   .   ]

—and sends a clerk with it into Lloyd's underwriters' room. This is an exceedingly large apartment, or rather series of apartments, down each of which run four rows of tables like those in an old-fashioned hotel coffee-room,—one row against each wall, and a double row down the middle; thus two side aisles give access, right and left, to two rows of tables. Each table is ceiled off from its neighbour by a partition about five feet high, so as to secure a certain degree of privacy, and each table accommodates four gentlemen. To enable a gentleman or firm to engage in the business of an underwriter, he must satisfy the committee which manages the room (usually by a considerable deposit, formerly £10,000, now, I believe, £5,000) that he is a person of adequate means to incur the risks of the business.

In this case the person applying to the broker wishes to insure the steamship *Sunshine* for £5,500, for a voyage from the Clyde to Hong-Kong, and he and the firm of brokers consider that 70s. per £100 is an adequate premium for the risk, and these particulars, and the date of the transaction and the name of the firm, are all noted on the slip, above the double line I have drawn across it. This slip is then sent into the room by the hand of one of his clerks. The clerk goes from table to table, and submits his slip to first one, and then another; some decline it, others append their initials as accepting, and write also, or the clerk does, the amounts which they are willing to insure. The broker himself insures nothing; his profit consists in deducting from the premium which he receives from the ship-owner or freighter, to hand over in the several proportions to the underwriters, a commission amounting to 15 per cent. on the several amounts, 5 per cent. of which he keeps, and 10 per cent. he returns to his employer in the matter. The particulars of the slip are then formally set forth in a policy of insurance, and each of the persons who have agreed to insure then formally subscribe or *underwrite* the body of the policy (hence the term " underwriters"), and receives from the broker 3½ per cent. on the respective amounts they had thus guaranteed to the owners of the ship in the event of her being lost.

In case of loss, the broker then applies to each of the gentlemen who have signed the policy for the respective sums they have each guaranteed, and the transaction is complete ; or the transaction is also completed by the safe arrival at Hong-Kong of the ship.

The next extract shows the policy, which was filled up from the slip already shown. In this case the whole of the sum insured is £5,500, and the risk is divided amongst forty-five subscribers (underwriters), not one of whom loses more than £150, while twenty-five only lose £100 each, in the event of the loss of the ship :—

[

S. G.

£5500

Delivered the   day
of   186 .

(*No.*   )

Be it known that   & *Co.*,

as well in *their* * own Name, as for and in the Name and Names of all and every other Person or Persons to whom the same doth, may, or shall appertain, in part or in all, doth make assurance and cause *themselves* and them and every of them, to be insured, lost or not lost, at and from *Clyde to Hong-Kong, and for and during the space of* 30 *consecutive days after arrival, with leave to take trial trip and to proceed to Gareloch to adjust compasses, and to call at all and any ports or places on the voyage for all and any purposes,* upon any Kind of Goods and Merchandises, and also upon the Body, Tackle, Apparel, Ordnance, Munition, Artillery, Boat and other Furniture, of and in the good Ship or Vessel called the *Sunshine* (*s.s.*), whereof is Master, under God, for this present Voyage

or whosoever else shall go for Master in the said Ship, or by whatsoever other Name or Names the same Ship, or the Master thereof, is or shall be named or called, beginning the Adventure upon the said Goods and Merchandise from the loading thereof aboard the said Ship

upon the said Ship, &c.

and shall so continue and endure, during her Abode there, upon the said Ship, &c. ; and further, until the said Ship, with all her Ordnance, Tackle, Apparel, &c., and Goods

---

* The words in italics represent the MS. portions of the Policy.

and Merchandise whatsoever, shall be arrived at [*as above*],

upon the said Ship, &c., until she hath moored at Anchor Twenty-four Hours in good Safety, and upon the Goods and Merchandises until the same be there discharged and safely landed ; and it shall be lawful for the said Ship, &c., in this Voyage to proceed and Sail to and touch and stay at any Ports or Places whatsoever *and wheresoever, and* without Prejudice to this Insurance. The said Ship, &c., Goods and Merchandise, &c., for so much as concerns the Assured, by Agreement between the Assured and Assurers in this Policy, are and shall be valued at £5,500 *on Hull and Machinery,* &c., *valued* £15,000 *average, payable on each value or lien separately over the whole general average, as per foreign statement, if so made up, including the collision clause, as attached.* Touching the Adventures and Perils which we, the Assurers, are contented to bear and do take upon us in this Voyage, they are, of the Seas, Men-of-War, Fire, Enemies, Pirates, Rovers, Thieves, Jettisons, Letters of Mart and Countermart, Surprisals, Takings at Sea, Arrests, Restraints and Detainments of all Kings, Princes, and People, of what Nation, Condition, or Quality soever, Barretry of the Master and Mariners, and of all other Perils, Losses, and Misfortunes that have or shall come to the Hurt, Detriment, or Damage of the said Goods and Merchandises and Ship, &c., or any Part thereof; and in case of any Loss or Misfortune it shall be lawful to the Assured, their Factors, Servants, and Assigns, to sue, labour, and travel for, in and about the Defence, Safeguard, and Recovery of the said Goods and Merchandises and Ship, &c., or any Part thereof, without Prejudice to this Insurance ; to the Charges whereof we, the Assurers, will contribute each one according to the Rate and Quantity of his Sum herein assured. And it is agreed by us, the Insurers, that this Writing or Policy of Assurance shall be of as much Force and Effect as the surest Writing or Policy of Assurance heretofore made in Lombard Street, or in the Royal Exchange, or elsewhere in London. And so we the Assurers are contented, and do hereby promise and bind ourselves, each one for his own Part, our Heirs, Executors, and Goods, to the Assured, their Executors, Administrators, and Assigns, for the true Performance of the Premises, confessing ourselves paid the Consideration due unto us for this Assurance by the Assured   at and after the Rate of *Seventy shillings per cent.*

IN WITNESS whereof, we the Assurers have subscribed our Names and Sums assured in *London,* 14 *Sept.,* 1869.

N.B.—Corn, Fish, Salt, Fruit, Flour, and Seed, are warranted free from Average, unless general, or the Ship be stranded ; Sugar, Tobacco, Hemp, Flax, Hides, and Skins are warranted free from Average under Five Pounds per

Cent.; and all other Goods, also the Ship and Freight, are warranted free from Average under Three Pounds per Cent., unless general, or the Ship be stranded.

[Here follow Signatures of Underwriters.]

Now, when you consider that the maximum loss to each person in this case is only £150, and consider the expense and worry of an investigation and trial in case of fraudulent carelessness, you will see that it is vain to expect any one of them to move alone, and a consideration of the difficulties in the way of combined action even amongst railway or bank shareholders to investigate and punish wrong-doing by directors shows also that nothing is to be expected from combined action.

But you may say, so far as unseaworthiness at least is concerned, inquiry previous to the insuring would reveal that: why don't the underwriters make this inquiry?—also, why don't they investigate the character of the proposed insurer? The answer is, the risk must be accepted or declined on the instant; and even if this were not so, the number of risks dealt with daily by each individual underwriter precludes this. To convince you of this, I now quote a page from the book in which an underwriter enters his engagements; it has been kindly lent me by the owner. (See next page.)

You see in this that the number dealt with by him in one day is more than twenty; the average in the book per day is twenty-three; and I am sure he will excuse me for saying that there are very many who deal with far greater numbers. Now, this is exclusive of all those (even more numerous) risks offered to him daily which he did not accept.

What chance was there that he should make inquiry into all these cases, even if there was time? He could not do it. All he could do he did,—*i.e.*, he referred to Lloyd's list, or the list of the Committee of Liverpool, and saw how the vessel was classed. I shall explain this further on.

I now show you another policy. The proposal is

24th JANUARY.				This column, referring to the nature of the cargoes, is nearly illegible.					
Lynwindon.	Annie Barker.	Lp.	Cienfuegos.		35/0	100	100	100	
	Saladin.	"	Pernamco.		15/0	100	100	100	
G. Tyser.	Trevelyan.	Melbourne.	Lon.		25/0	50	50	50	
J. M'Andrews.	" 1 per.	Lon.	Bordeaux.		7/6	150	150	150	
Stock, W.	Mira Flores.	Lpool.	Conste.		15/0	40	30	30	
Haycraft.	"	Clyde.	Valpo.		25/0	20	20	20	
Bischoff & Co.	S. B. " 10 per.	Marslles. & Genoa.	N. York, &c.		30/0	50	50	50	
" "	" " "	" "	" " "		15/0	100	100	100	
Roxburghe.	Scandinavian.	Lpool.	Portld, &c.		"	100	30	30	
" "	S. B. 26 Jan.	"	"		12/6	40	100	100	
Rose, T.	Ships. 5 per.	Nfland.	Europe.		"	100	100	100	
Lourdes and R.	" 10 per.	Calar.	N. Yk. & Boston.		25/0	200	200	200	
Maclean.	Dcca, 3. 26 per.	12 months.	"		30/0	100	100	100	
C. S. Whealler.	Ships. 25 per.	China.	Nu.		7 gs.	200	200	200	
Rose, T.	Glenallan. 7 per.	12 months.			45/0	100	100	100	
Fenning.	Trent.	Lon.	Colon.		7 gs.	200	200	200	
Cotton.	Seaman.	Burmah.	Lon.		22/6	100	100	100	
Linawide.	Nelson.	Lon.	Consple.		12/6	100	100	100	
Rose, T.	Appendix.	B. Ayres.	U. K.		7/6	100	100	100	B. India.
					40/0	100	100	100	

Note.—If any technical inaccuracies occur in the above table, they must be attributed to the extreme difficulty in deciphering many of the words and contractions. In any case, the purpose required by the text will be served.—*The Publishers.*

by a firm called "F. C. & Co." on the slip, to effect
an insurance on £50,000 worth of cotton to be bought
in Bombay, and to be sent home U. K. (United Kingdom) in such quantities and in such ships as their
agent in Bombay may determine. In this case the rate
offered is 50*s.* per £100, and the risk is accepted at that
rate in various amounts. You will see the policy which
was executed in accordance with the terms implied rather
than specified on the slip. This policy was underwritten
by 118 individuals,—

67 of whom guaranteed	£500	each	=	£33,500
25	,,	,,	400	=	10,000
11	,,	,,	300	=	3,300
4	,,	,,	250	=	1,000
and 11	,,	,,	200	=	2,200
	In all .	.	.	.	£50,000

But as the quantity was sent home in five ships, the *Cher-
well*, the *Bavelaw*, the *British Flag*, the *Oberon*, and the
British Peer, the highest risk to each underwriter per ship
was only £100, and to the lowest only £40.

[No. CCCXVIII.

& Co.'s Lloyd's Policy.

Be it known that   *& Co.,*

For as agents

S. G.

£50,000.

Delivered the   day
of

(*No.*   )

as well in *their* own Name, as for and in the
Name and Names of all and every other
Person or Persons to whom the same doth,
may, or shall appertain, in part or in all,
doth make assurance and cause *themselves*
and them and every of them, to be insured,
lost or not lost, at and from *Bombay to any
port or ports of call for discharge in the
United Kingdom. With leave to call at all
ports and places as well on this as at and on
the other side of the Cape of Good Hope for
any and all purposes*, upon any Kind of Goods and Merchandises, and also upon the Body, Tackle, Apparel, Ord-

nance, Munition, Artillery, Boat and other Furniture, of and in the good Ship or Vessel called the
"*Ship*" or "*Ships*,"
whereof is Master, under God for this present Voyage,
or whosoever else shall go for Master in the said Ship, or by whatsoever other Name or Names the same Ship, or the Master thereof, is or shall be named or called, beginning the Adventure upon the said Goods and Merchandises from the loading thereof aboard the said Ship

upon the said Ship, &c., *including all risk of craft in loading and discharging,* and shall so continue and endure, during her Abode there, upon the said Ship, &c.; and further, until the said Ship, with all her Ordnance, Tackle, Apparel, &c., and Goods and Merchandises whatsoever, shall be arrived at

upon the said Ship, &c., until she hath moored at Anchor Twenty-four Hours in good Safety, and upon the Goods and Merchandises until the same be there discharged and safely landed; and it shall be lawful for the said Ship, &c., in this Voyage to proceed and sail to and touch and stay at any Ports or Places whatsoever *and wheresoever, for any and all purposes, without being deemed a deviation, and* without Prejudice to this Insurance. The said Ship, &c., Goods and Merchandises, &c., for so much as concerns the Assured, by Agreement between the Assured and Assurers in this Policy, are and shall be valued at £50,000, *on Cotton, as Interest may appear or as may be declared and valued hereafter. To pay average as customary. General average payable as per foreign statement if so made up.* Touching the Adventures and Perils which we the Assurers are contented to bear and do take upon us in this Voyage, they are, of the Seas, Men-of-War, Fire, Enemies, Pirates, Rovers, Thieves, Jettisons, Letters of Mart and Countermart, Surprisals, Takings at Sea, Arrests, Restraints and Detainments of all Kings, Princes, and People, of what Nation, Condition, or Quality soever, Barretry of the Master and Mariners, and of all other Perils, Losses, and Misfortunes that have or shall come to the Hurt, Detriment, or Damage of the said Goods and Merchandises and Ship, &c., or any Part thereof; and in case of any Loss or Misfortune it shall be lawful to the Assured, their Factors, Servants, and Assigns, to sue, labour, and travel for, in, and about the Defence, Safeguard, and Recovery of the said Goods and Merchandises and Ship, &c., or any Part thereof, without Prejudice to this Insurance; to the Charges whereof we, the Assurers, will contribute each one according to the Rate and Quantity of his Sum herein assured. And it is agreed by us, the Insurers, that this Writing or Policy of Assurance shall be of as much Force and Effect as the surest Writing or Policy of Assurance heretofore made in Lombard Street, or in the Royal Exchange, or elsewhere in London. And so we the Assurers are contented, and do hereby promise and bind

ourselves, each one for his own Part, our Heirs, Executors, and Goods, to the Assured, their Executors, Administrators, and Assigns, for the true Performance of the Premises, confessing ourselves paid the Consideration due unto us for this Assurance by the Assured
at and after the Rate of *Fifty shillings per cent. To return 9/6 o/o for interest sailing between 20 Oct. and 20 April, and 4/9 o/o for vessels 10 years A 1 and upwards, and arrival.*

Warranted free from capture and seizure and the consequences of any attempt thereat.

IN WITNESS whereof, we the Assurers have subscribed our names and Sums assured in *London, 2 April,* 1869.

N.B.—Corn, Fish, Salt, Fruit, Flour, and Seed are warranted free from Average, unless general, or the Ship be stranded; Sugar, Tobacco, Hemp, Flax, Hides, and Skins are warranted free from Average under Five Pounds per Cent.; and all other Goods, also the Ship and Freight, are warranted free from Average under Three Pounds per Cent., unless general, or the Ship be stranded.

It is agreed that this Policy shall cover all cotton belonging to Ritchie, Steuart & Co., of Bombay, or which they may receive instructions to insure. Shipments to attach in order as declared, and any shipments not declared to attach according to dates of Bills of Lading, but after declarations already made.
Declarations in all cases to be made binding as to the value of the Interest, or in the absence of them the Rupee of Invoice to be taken at 2s. 3d., including premium and all charges for insurance. To follow and succeed a Policy for £50,000, etc., done at Lloyd's and dated 19 *March,* 1869.
Warranted to sail on or before 31 *Dec.,* 1869.

[*Here follow the Signatures of the Underwriters.*]   ]

The next quotation illustrates a third slip—they have all been taken, as you see, for large amounts, in order to show how the responsibility, even in these cases, is so divided and spread as to leave no one individual a risk large enough to be worth fighting to escape, even if there were adequate grounds for disputing the subsequent claim.

In this case, the proposal is to insure purchases of cotton in Bombay to the amount of £10,000, to be sent home (U. K.) in such ships and quantities as the proposer's agent in Bombay might determine, as the purchases were made:

50*s.* per £100 is the rate broker and insurer agree to offer, and it is subscribed at that premium.

The particulars in all these cases are given in the way shown on page 13.

Here is the policy which resulted :—

[

S. G.
———————————
£10,000.
———————————
Delivered the   day)
of   }

(*No.*   )

Be it known that   *& Co.,*

as well in *their* own name, as for and in the Name and Names of all and every other Person or Persons to whom the same doth, may, or shall appertain, in part or in all, doth make assurance and cause *themselves* and them and every of them, to be insured, lost or not lost, at and from *Bombay to a Port of call for discharge in the United Kingdom. With leave to call at all and any Ports and Places on the Voyage, for all and any purposes,* upon any Kind of Goods and Merchandises, and also upon the Body, Tackle, Apparel, Ordnance, Munition, Artillery, Boat and other Furniture, of and in the good Ship or Vessel called the

" Ship " or " Ships,"

warranted to sail on or before 30*th June,* 1869, whereof is Master, under God for this present Voyage, or whosoever else shall go for Master in the said Ship, or by whatsoever other Name or Names the same Ship, or the Master thereof, is or shall be named or called, beginning the Adventure upon the said Goods and Merchandises from the loading thereof aboard the said Ship

upon the said Ship, &c., *including all risk of craft to and from the vessel,* and shall so continue and endure, during her Abode there, upon the said Ship, &c. ; and further, until the said Ship, with all her Ordnance, Tackle, Apparel, &c., and Goods and Merchandises whatsoever, shall be arrived at

upon the said Ship, &c., until she hath moored at Anchor Twenty-four Hours in good Safety, and upon the Goods and Merchandises until the same be there discharged and safely landed ; and it shall be lawful for the said Ship, &c., in this Voyage to proceed and sail to and touch and stay at any Ports or Places whatsoever *and wheresoever, for all and any purposes, without being deemed a deviation, and* without Prejudice to this Insurance. The said Ship, &c., Goods and Merchandises, &c., for so much as concerns the Assured, by Agreement between the Assured and Assurers in this Policy, are and shall be valued at £10,000, *on Cotton, as may be hereafter declared and valued. Being on shipments made by Stenhouse & Co., of Bombay, in which they are interested ; or which they may have received instructions to insure.*

Touching the Adventures and Perils which we the Assurers are contented to bear and do take upon us in this Voyage, they are, of the Seas, Men-of-War, Fire, Enemies, Pirates, Rovers, Thieves, Jettisons, Letters of Mart and Countermart, Surprisals, Takings at Sea, Arrests, Restraints and Detainments of all Kings, Princes, and People, of what Nation, Condition, or Quality soever, Barretry of the Master and Mariners, and of all other Perils, Losses, and Misfortunes that have or shall come to the Hurt, Detriment, or Damage of the said Goods and Merchandises and Ship, &c., or any Part thereof; and in case of any Loss or Misfortune it shall be lawful to the Assured, their Factors, Servants, and Assigns, to sue, labour, and travel for, in, and about the Defence, Safeguard, and Recovery of the said Goods and Merchandises and Ship, &c., or any Part thereof, without Prejudice to this Insurance; to the Charges whereof we, the Assurers, will contribute each one according to the Rate and Quantity of his Sum herein assured. And it is agreed by us, the Insurers, that this Writing or Policy of Assurance shall be of as much Force and Effect as the surest Writing or Policy of Assurance heretofore made in Lombard Street, or in the Royal Exchange, or elsewhere in London. And so we the Assurers are contented, and do hereby promise and bind ourselves, each one for his own Part, our Heirs, Executors, and Goods, to the Assured, their Executors, Administrators, and Assigns, for the true Performance of the Premises, confessing ourselves paid the Consideration due unto us for this Assurance by the Assured
at and after the Rate of *Fifty Shillings per Cent. To return* 9/6 o/o *for sailing between* 20th October and 20th April; and 4/6 o/o *for Interest in Ships* A 1, 10 *years and upwards, and arrival.*

IN WITNESS whereof, we the Assurers have subscribed our Names and Sums assured in *London,* 31st December, 1868.

N.B.—Corn, Fish, Salt, Fruit, Flour, and Seed are warranted free from Average, unless general, or the Ship be stranded; Sugar, Tobacco, Hemp, Flax, Hides, and Skins are warranted free from Average under Five Pounds per Cent.; and all other Goods, also the Ship and Freight, are warranted free from Average under Three Pounds per Cent., unless general, or the Ship be stranded.

To follow and succeed a Policy for £10,000, done at Lloyd's, and dated 30th *July,* 1868.
To pay average on every 10 *Bales running landing numbers.*
General Average, payable as per foreign statement, if so made up.
Declarations to be made binding in their order, whether in the order of the Bills of Lading or otherwise; or in the absence of Declarations, they shall be in the order of the Date of the Bills of Lading. Declarations in all cases to be bind-

ing as to the value of the Interest; and in the absence of them, the Rupee of the Invoice to be taken at 2s. 3d.; to include Premium and all charges for Insurance.

[Here follow the Signatures of the Underwriters.]   **]**

In this case the policy was signed , by 58 persons, of whom—

34 signed for £200 each	=	£6,800
16	„	150	=	2,400
and 8	„	100	=	800

In all £10,000

But here the cotton was put into eight ships, so that the highest risk to each underwriter was per ship only £25, whilst to the others it was only £12 10s.

These are not paltry cases. The sums (£50,000, £10,000, and £5,500) assured are all large ; yet, in these large cases it will be seen that the individual payment in case of loss was far too small to induce any one to fight a lawsuit in order to escape it.

But, besides the reason that the individual loss of an underwriter is too small, considering the trouble and expense, to make it worth his while to dispute a claim,

He is not strong enough.

Consider how the relative positions of insurer and insured differ here between the case of a ship being insured and that of a factory or warehouse. In the latter case, those called upon to pay are the stronger far of the two parties. It is a company with skilled advisers and organised staff, with solicitors and a watchful executive, against the resources of an individual. In the case we are considering it is an individual only who is called upon to pay, and the claim is made by a powerful firm, or wealthy individual ship-owner—or even if not very wealthy, yet one possessing a tremendous stake in the matter, and who may therefore be confidently expected to spare no effort or exertion in prosecuting it. The claimant has the whole amount of the loss at stake, the underwriter only an insignificant portion of it.

What wonder is it then that the issue is, as it nearly inva-
riably is, that the claim is paid ? with much grumbling sometimes, it may be, and sometimes with more than a suspicion
of its injustice.   Still, it is paid, and the only remedial measure open to the underwriter is, that if he has good grounds
for suspicion, he merely makes a mental note to have no
further dealings with the suspected persons.   As a matter
of fact, almost all claims, no matter how founded in fraud,
are thus paid, and it is the rarest thing in the world (it does
not occur once in 50,000 cases) that a claim is disputed.
You can judge also, by this, how wretchedly bad the case
of a ship-owner is, who, to reflections of an injurious nature
upon such and such a case, can only urge, as proof that all
was as it should be, the plea that " the underwriters have
not disputed, but have paid, his claim."

A further reason why an underwriter cannot dispute a claim
consists in the fact, that to do so after taking the premium
(and surely no one expects others to meddle) is probably to
expose his motive to great *suspicion*, and certainly to expose
his conduct to the most painful and odious *misrepresentation.*
"What!" cries the indignant policy-holder, "you said nothing about ship or cargo when the broker paid you the premium ; you were quiet enough then ; and now, when you are
called upon to pay the sum you insured, on some cock-and-
bull story you have heard, or some letter you have received,
or certain information you *say* you have received, you dispute the matter—not, of course," he adds with withering
sarcasm, "that you are anxious about the money !   It is
merely in the interests of justice !   You are merely animated
by a sense of public duty ! "

Who can expect a man to incur all this odious misrepresentation and suspicion, when he can escape it all by paying
the comparatively small sum demanded of him?

He knows, too (and this is a fourth reason), that to dispute such a claim is at once and *completely to end his career
as an underwriter*, and this, too, even if the brokers through
whom future business is to come are fully satisfied that he

did right, that the disputed claim was founded in fraud, and
that his motives were pure ; and further, that if he had succeeded, a wrong-doer would only have met his deserts.

You say, " How should this be ?" Well, in this way. The
insurance broker has no pecuniary interest in the matter either
way. He procures for the ship-owner the guarantee he wants,
and the event insured against having happened, his only wish
is to get it settled as soon as possible. He, too, may have
made his mental note of the case adverse to further business with his customer, but at present his only concern is to
get the matter settled as quickly as possible. But if one of
the signatories to the policy refuses to pay, others may do
so too (some of them have paid already, and this supplies
our indignant wrecker with a strong point, " These men
have paid—these men are honourable. *They* don't take a
man's premium, and then try to evade their responsibility,"
&c., &c.) With some of the money in hand, and with
others, who would have paid had not one underwriter pro-
tested, what is the broker to do ? He has, it will be admitted, a most troublesome business to settle somehow ; and
who can wonder, then, that in negotiating fresh business in
the Room, and to avoid future complications, he prefers that
his slips shall be · signed, his proposals accepted by those
who will pay in the event of loss without raising inconvenient objections, leaving the remedy for wrong to time,
and the resource of avoiding the business of such a person
again.

Now, that this is the remedy, and the only remedy, available and adopted by underwriters, perhaps the following
extract from a pamphlet published by one of them may
make more clear. The writer complains, it will be seen, of
the great difficulty, amounting almost to impossibility, of
getting even an error in the claim rectified :—

[Now, I know that in starting my argument for carrying these measures
into effect, I shall at the outset be opposed by that very respectable but
antiquated bugbear—" Individuality of action." But I fear I am
somewhat sceptical of its existence in the Room, except in a homœo-
pathic quantity ; and if it does exist, I also doubt if it is used in such a

way as to add to the prestige of Lloyd's, or bring more business into the Room. Certainly, premiums are incessantly being nibbled at and reduced; losses and claims that should not be settled are very frequently settled, while others that should be settled at once are often delayed. *In our business we daily submit to being defrauded on all sides,. and yet have contented ourselves, very often, with merely lamenting the fact, instead of combining to cope with so great an evil. But perhaps combination and centralisation are incompatible with individuality of action, and, if so, of course they merit the opposition with which they have been so often treated.*

To show my meaning, I will assume a case of frequent occurrence. *A claim is brought before an Underwriter, and on examining it he finds it incorrect—say in principle. The first few men on the policy may have settled it, either because they have not had time to look into it, or because the account it occurs on is such a good one they do not like to raise any questions, or perhaps because they do not understand it, therefore cannot check it. In such a case it too often happens that the policy is settled over the heads of the man who has discovered the error and perhaps others with him, and then brought back to them in such a way as to place them in a very invidious position; or else, as sometimes happens, the settlement is asked as a favour; and at any rate one feels the uselessness of contesting even a flagrant case, when the majority of settlements on the policy will be brought against one as evidence in court, and a jury would be nearly certain to argue that the others would not have settled had the claim been incorrect, and would, in nine cases out of ten, give their verdict accordingly.* But in such a case, where is the individuality of action? and if you find it, what good did it do? You may ask, why did the Average Staters make up the claim? and I would answer by asking you, are not the Average Staters as liable to competition as any of us, and are they not frequently pressed to insert in their statements claims for which the Underwriters are not liable? They know that if they refuse, there are other Average Staters who will do it, and so they may lose their business connection by their want of compliance, and get no credit from the Underwriters either, as of course the latter cannot know what has happened in such a case.   ]

It will be seen that the writer complains of want of com-bination as the source of the weakness of underwriters. I should be running a risk of leaving it open to doubt whether organisation would not be an effectual remedy, if I failed to point out that no organisation whatever would avail to secure proof in one case in one hundred of wrong-doing; for, as will be more fully seen further on, the proofs and the witnesses too in the greater part of the cases would be in the bottom of the sea. Now, that the remedy, and the only remedy available and adopted by underwriters, is caution in the future, I think I can show you. Permit a

digression. Ship-owners, as a class, are really careful of
their men's lives, and neglect no means of safety known to
them ; and that they are so, considering that the law leaves
them entirely free to neglect these means if they pleased, is
a fact very much to their credit. But there are in every
large class of men some who need the law's restraint—who,
without it, have no hesitation in exposing others to risk, if
by doing so they can augment their own profits ; amongst
these are the pushing and energetic, and sometimes needy
men. What wonder is it, therefore, if these, under the
pressure of competition and greed, should habitually decide
points, where the right and wrong are not very clearly
defined, in a sense favourable to themselves? Thus, suppose a ship will take 900 tons of cargo with safety, leaving
her side one-third as high out of water as it is deep below
it ; and suppose, further, that the freight of 700 tons is
absorbed by expenses—wages of seamen, cost of fuel, wear
and tear, interest of capital, cost of insurance, &c.—leaving
the freight on the remaining 200 tons as profit to the owner,
it is clear that by loading an additional 200 tons the profits
are doubled, while the load is only increased by about a
quarter more. And this addition will not load her so
deeply as to prevent her making a good voyage, if the
weather is favourable. What wonder is there, I say, that
needy or unscrupulous men adopt the larger load? They
are safe in any case.

If the vessel makes her port, they secure a very great
profit. If she meets with rough weather and is lost, they
recover her value (in too many instances far more than her
value), and so go on again.

Nor does the fear of losing the lives of the men operate
so greatly upon these men's minds as it would if it were
certain, or even probable, that in all cases where the ship
is lost the men would be lost too ; for so generally are
dangerous parts of the coast supplied with life-boats, and so
numerous are they and other means of saving life from
wrecks, such as the rocket brigades, the coast-guard service,

and the fishing-boats, that no less than five-sixths of the men who are wrecked, and whose lives (so far as the ships in which they sailed are concerned) are lost—five-sixths of these are saved by these means. So that such men know that if their ship is lost *on our coasts*, the chances that the men will be saved are as five to one.

Under these circumstances, it is not surprising that a few men are found amongst ship-owners who are not unwilling to expose their men to this diminished risk, where the gains of overloading are so large and the risk to themselves nothing at all.

It need not be said that such men have frequent losses— indeed, the losses we deplore are nearly all of this class; and I have heard one ship-owner say that if a small number of well-known ship-owners were put aboard one of their own vessels when she was ready for sea, we should, in the event of bad weather, see that with them had disappeared from our annals nine-tenths of the losses we all deplore.   .

But to return : I was to show you that the only remedy of an underwriter against these men is the purpose of declining their business in future.

This is so ; and, in particular instances, such is the evil reputation which some bad men acquire, so generally are they known for their habitual overloading, for their terribly frequent and disastrous losses, for their cynical disregard of human life, that after paying increasingly high rates of premium for insurance, in the ports where they are known, the time sometimes comes when they can only insure in London, where they are as yet unknown, and even there, after still further experience, their names become so black with infamy, that nobody will insure their risks at any premium, and where it is necessary in the course of business to insure cargo not yet purchased, as corn or cotton abroad, or not yet ready for delivery, as railroad iron for foreign, and when the ships are not taken up yet (in which case it is usual to say on the slip " in a ship or ships "), the brokers

dare not offer their slips in the Room, or would have no
chance of success if they did, unless they wrote under the
usual particulars these damning words—"Warranted not
to be shipped in any vessels belonging to —, —, —, —:"
the blanks being filled up with the names of certain ship-
owners; and I, Samuel Plimsoll, who am writing this letter,
say that I have seen slips so endorsed, and that too with
names which (however well known by a few) stand fair in
the eye of the world, in which their infamous owners hold
their heads very high indeed.

There is indeed one other remedy, but it is not often
available to an underwriter: it is when he has early information of wrong-doing after underwriting and before a
catastrophe. A case I knew of was that of Mr. ————,
insuring a part of a ship and cargo from India to England.
A letter happened to be posted to him in India the day
before the ship sailed; the letter arrived first; it stated that
"the ————, which sails to-morrow, is very deep in the
water; she is much overloaded." This underwriter immediately reinsured at Lloyd's, to cover his own risk. The
ship was lost; but the money he received from the other
underwriter covered his own loss: but this, you see, is a
mere shifting of the burden. Forgive me for taking so
much pains, and occupying so much of your time in clear-
ing up this point. I feel it to be of the utmost importance.
The current idea on the subject is an error, a fatal and
homicidal mistake, and surely no pains can be too great to
take, no expense too large to incur, to uproot it, and
impress the right view—consider, our object is to save
precious human life !

I earnestly hope that I have convinced you that it is vain
to expect an underwriter to interfere to mend matters,
because—his interest is too small; because—he is not
strong enough; because—he would expose himself to painful suspicion; and because—to do so would destroy his
business.

But even if we could find one sufficiently bold, public-spirited, and unselfish, as to be willing, notwithstanding all this, to take up the matter, consider what enormous difficulties would meet him at the very outset.

Suppose it was the case I have quoted of a ship sailing from India, which was lost from shameful overloading, and that instead of reinsuring the underwriter had decided to investigate the case, and bring it before a court of law. He must go or send a commission to India to collect evidence as to the state of the ship at the time of sailing (what time and expense are involved here !). Such evidence is frequently too general—the witness could not define precisely the depth to which the ship was loaded ; he wrote from general observation. Again, is the witness to be brought to England? As to the ship herself, she is at the bottom of the sea. The captain and seamen could no doubt give their opinions, but they too are at the bottom of the sea—clearly nothing could be done in this case.

Let us take a better : the ship is lost nearer home, captain and men are saved, but they have to work for a living, and before news of the loss is to hand, they have gone to their homes, or they are engaged in other ships, and are scattered over every sea.

Let us take another still easier for the underwriter, the case of a ship sailing from one of our own ports to another port also in England, and wrecked, let us say in Yarmouth Roads, the crew all saved—and let us suppose that our friend hears of the disaster immediately, and sets off for Yarmouth, first telegraphing for the men to wait his arrival.

He finds them, he employs legal assistance, their evidence is collected, the case is clear. What then ? They may be unwilling witnesses ; the captain, the officers, the men all know that if they give evidence they destroy their chances of future employment, even by owners who disapprove the practices of the owners of the lost ship. They have escaped with their lives, they hope for better luck next voyage; even if their late employer is punished, the bad system remains untouched; why should they sacrifice their

chances of future employment? Some of them indeed may
be bought over by the owner or agents—such people are
not likely to be very nice in their dealings. But we will
suppose none of these things happen, and the trial comes
on. What then? Why, the trial can only be taken in
turn or at assizes; the men must live in the meantime.
The underwriter takes on himself all the cost of maintaining
them in the interval—perhaps it is a long one—and the trial
at length takes place. What happens then? The owners
bring evidence too, and anybody knows how easy it is with
a long purse to obtain plausible or professional evidence
for even a bad cause. The chances are much against his
getting a verdict or otherwise gaining his cause, and, if he
does succeed, what will he have done by all this expenditure
of time and money? He will have secured that one bad
man was punished, and he will have destroyed himself as
an underwriter. Further, he will know that for the one man
punished hundreds go free, as in the great majority of cases
it would be impossible, even with all this impossible assump-
tion of energy and self-sacrifice, so much as to get evidence
enough to go into court with at all.

I am sorry to have taken so much of your time on this
point, but I trust that at least this result is made clear—
clear as a demonstration in mathematics—that it is vain to
expect a remedy from the underwriters.

Observe how not only different, but how opposite are all
the circumstances of insuring a factory and insuring a ship.

In insuring a house or a factory, the party to the contract
who has to pay the loss is the stronger of the two; in the
case of a ship, he is infinitely the weaker. If wrong-doing
is attempted in the former case, it is with risk of life to his
family in the case of a house, and with the greatest risk of
detection to himself in that of either house or warehouse;
in the latter, the owner of a ship may induce the result
simply by neglect—by indefinite postponement of repair.
In the former, if loss occur, it is known immediately; in
the latter, many months often intervene before the loss is

known.   In the former the proofs and the witnesses are on the spot; in the latter the proofs are at the bottom of the sea, and the witnesses, even if saved, are at the ends of the earth.

And yet, in the face of all this, we hear from a gentleman high in authority and influence, who could long since have extended to our seamen the protection they need, and which is enjoyed by all other classes of our fellow-subjects, words like these—read them for yourself :—

From the JOURNAL OF THE SOCIETY OF ARTS,
February 11, 1870.

[The next topic, that of deck-loading, was of considerable importance. Mr. Wood proposed that no dead weight of any description should be allowed, that no animal or other cargo should be carried on a steamer's bridge, &c.   Now, to interfere with the loading of a ship was to interfere with the business of a ship-owner, and if you did that at all, it would only be logical to do so entirely.   Again, by making such a provision, you would virtually shut up certain classes of trade altogether.   As one instance with which he was familiar, he might mention the steamers that plied from Glasgow round the Hebrides and Orkneys and to Wick.   They were really steam omnibuses.   They touched at one place, perhaps, and took in a few bags of periwinkles; at another a few bags of meal and a sheep or two; then at another island they would deposit the sheep to graze, and exchange the meal for salt fish, and so on through the whole journey.   If these steamers could not carry cargo on deck their trade would be stopped altogether.   Again, if such a law were made, it would easily be defeated.   They would only have to put an awning deck above, which would be kept clear, and then they would carry even more than at present on the deck, and so perhaps render the boats more unsafe than they are alleged to be at present.   He did not think Government ought to interfere in any way in the carrying or stowing of cargo, which must be understood and performed better by the ship-owner than by any Government agent. With regard to overloading and load-lines, the object with which keels carrying coals were first marked, was purely a fiscal one.   The vessel was loaded down to a certain line, and nails were then driven in at the stem and stern to show how much cargo she was to carry; she was taxed for that amount, and was not allowed to carry more.   In the same way the registration of tonnage was required purely for fiscal purposes.   A register ton simply meant 100 cubic feet of internal space, and the object of fixing it was to apportion the light dues to be paid by each vessel.   It had nothing whatever to do with the carrying capacity or the load-line.   The formula given by Mr. Moorsom, as quoted in the paper, was only offered as a rough-and-ready method, as stated by that gentleman, because some owners were unwilling to take the trouble of making the necessary deductions alluded to.   With regard to a load-line, all he could say was that in 1853 the Board of Trade consulted a number of practical persons throughout the country on this subject, and the result was they could not get any two persons to agree as to the method of calculating such a load-line; but Mr. Wood now proposed that there should be two, according to the quality of the cargo, which would greatly increase the difficulty. There would be immediate complications if the vessel carried a cargo partly composed of one kind of goods and partly of another, and the load-line must vary according to the proportions. The real remedy appeared to him to be this, that the Government, instead of interfering in any way with the loading, should see that on both stem and stern the correct draught of water was placed. A record would then be kept of the draught of water of all ships going to sea, and it would rest with the parties interested to see whether any ship went to sea properly loaded or not. The proposal, that the collector of customs should detain a master's certificate because his vessel was overloaded appeared specially objectionable, as it made the captain suffer for the fault of the owner. With regard to lifeboats and rafts, he considered they were exceedingly necessary, but he feared British ship-owners would never be persuaded to carry a raft instead of a boat (though in a big ship it might be carried as well), because the one could be used for ordinary purposes and the other could not. The last thing to be done, therefore, was to provide such a boat as should be available both for ordinary purposes and also for saving life in case of accident. The matter under discussion was but one part, and that a small one, of a very large question. Prevention, it was well known, was better than cure, and prevention in some shape must be looked to; the only question was how it could be applied. Some people wished to prevent loss of life by inspections, certificates, and Government interference, whilst another mode was to abolish Government interference altogether, and to leave the owner responsible for his own acts and to make him pay in the event of culpable neglect or any abuse of the power entrusted to him. Take the case of railways; he did not believe that if a Board of Trade official were to inspect every line of railway daily, sit on every engine and watch it, be at every signal-post, and smell every man's breath to make sure he was not drunk, there would be so few accidents as under the present system, by which heavy damages were given against railway companies in case of accidents. Let a ship-owner do his business and mind his business, and let the underwriters and Government do the same. *Let ships be lost and cargoes be lost, so long as underwriters are too sordid or too lazy to refuse payment of doubtful and fraudulent cases.* But if the ship-owner puts the country to expense, or causes or contributes to the death of a citizen, let him have justice without mercy. It was precisely the same with the owner of a mine. He had just been talking to the owner of a large mine in the north, who told him he had just had a boiler blown up. He inquired how that came to happen, and he said he did not know; the overlooker inspected it every week, the under-overlooker every day, and it was also insured in the Boiler Association, on whose behalf it was also inspected regularly. It had been inspected and repaired only three days before it blew up, and the inspector congratulated him on having so good a boiler. Again, all the men had lamps, which were inspected by men in his own employment, who were responsible. If all this were done by a Government inspector it would not be done so well, and the responsibility would be shifted from the right shoulders to the wrong ones. The evil of modern legislation had been that it was, to a great extent, sensational. When the *Cricket* blew up, everybody said what a horrible thing it was, and that explosions must be prevented, and the consequence was that legislation was undertaken in a panic, and that was the basis of the Steam Navigation Act, and of parts of the Shipping Act, and he was afraid to say how long the system would be perpetuated. People had a superstitious idea that because a ship had been inspected she must be safe ; if they could only get over that superstition and apply the proper remedy, he believed many difficulties would be removed, and there would soon be a diminution in the loss of life at sea. He confined himself to the question of loss of life, because, of course, property must look after itself. He could hardly do better than conclude by quoting a passage from Herbert Spencer :—" Ever since society has existed, disappointment has been preaching put not your trust in legislation, and yet our trust in legislation is scarcely diminished. We have long since ceased to coerce men for their spiritual good, though we have not yet ceased to coerce them for their temporal good, not seeing that the one is as useless and unwarrantable as the other."]

" *Inebriate, clinging to lamppost :* ' What am I staying here for ? Why,—hic—don't you see that the street is— hic—turnin' roun' and roun'? Well, then,—hic—I'm waiting till my house comes opposite, and then I'll—hic— go in.' "

I have suppressed the name of the speaker, because, for aught I know, the special knowledge which could have served him, and so saved thousands of lives, was probably not required of him on his appointment, and if that was so, it would not be reasonable to complain of his not possessing it ; but I do consider there is very great cause of complaint in the promise exacted by him from a deputation o f working men, which waited upon the President of the Board of Trade last year, to urge upon him that measures should be taken by Government to protect the lives of their fellow working men at sea.

The deputation was numerous, and consisted of delegates from nearly all the large inland manufacturing towns, and we counted greatly upon the moral effect of the deputation, and what the members of it had to say, upon public opinion.

Well, before a word was said, this gentleman asked if any reporters were present? There was no official reporter ; one of the deputation was a contributor to the press, and we relied upon him ; but we were told we could not be heard, unless we would engage that no report of the meeting should be made to the press.   We were greatly disappointed, but there was no appeal, and, hoping to impress the President's mind sufficiently for our purpose, we acquiesced.

I afterwards noticed that Mr. Gladstone and the Home Secretary, or Mr. Forster (I forget which of the two latter names), at any rate two Cabinet Ministers, received two deputations the same day, and the following day full reports, both of the names of the deputation and what they had to say, appeared in the papers, doubtless to the advantage of their respective causes.   Now, why should the working men, so disinterestedly working for the sailors, have been denied the enormous advantage to their cause of publicity ?

I am afraid that the Marine Department of the Board of Trade is uncomfortably conscious that things are wrong, but don't see their way to a remedy, and don't want to be disturbed.

There seems to be a good deal of energy there too (if only it were more wisely directed), for recently the wreck charts, always very good and full of information (they tabulate results well, but don't see the fearful lessons they should teach), have appeared in all the glories of chromolithography, and the ghastly results appear gay with red, blue, buff, yellow, green, and black (making it impossible to get a good negative), a proceeding which suggests the idea of a homicide smitten with lunacy, and decking the body of his victim with flowers.   For Heaven's sake, while we have to publish such fearful figures, let us do it decently again, in black.

To resume, however.   I trust I have shown you that we cannot look, with any reason or probability for any remedy to existing abuses, to the underwriters.

Sailors.—Can we, with any better hope of success, look to the sailors themselves ?   Cannot they refuse to sail except in ships so sound, so efficiently equipped, and so properly loaded, as to satisfy all reasonable expectations and to afford a fair chance of their making a safe voyage ? Well, you have to consider their circumstances before you can form a sound opinion on this point. The sailor is not given to calculating too nicely all probable dangers any more than other working men; indeed, it may be safely said that if working men did thus stay to calculate their chances of safety, half the work of the world would remain undone. It is not a labour free from danger to life and limb to build a lofty pile of warehouses : a false step when near the top, the least unsteadiness of eye or hand, the momentary failing of their nerve, a badly-tied scaffold cord, and they meet with a violent death. This is still more the case in the building of a steeple or chimney-stack. It is dreadfully injurious to health to grind forks, and the late Dr. Holland showed that few dry grinders lived to be more than thirty-one years of age. Yet there has never been a lack of men willing and ready to engage in any of these occupations. To be engaged upon the building of a bridge, to earn your living by descending into the sewers of London, and spending the long day in an atmosphere so foul that a light will scarcely burn, are not pursuits tending to long life. Yet men are found to do all this. To sink a shaft hundreds of yards deep, and work in it day by day for months, where a bit of stone, falling from the top, or from an ascending load, is almost certain death, would not attract a man thoughtful about risks and desirous of long life. There are many employments almost certainly fatal to life after a longer or shorter time, and which are plentifully productive of ill health during life, but there is no lack of candidates even for these. To spend your life underground in a mine or in a coal-pit, far away from the pit bottom, and where the dangers increase in proportion to the number employed, for *each* man holds the lives of *all* the rest in his keeping, and the safety of *all* depends upon the care with which *each single man* guards his light—this, surely, is not a life free from peril, leaving out of consideration the danger of tapping some old working, and so letting in death as a flood upon them.

Yet, for all these employments there are always men ready and waiting. The simple fact is that working men

have no choice, their own needs are pressing, their wives
and children look to them for bread ; while they hesitate (if
they do hesitate) they hunger, and so, as each man thinks
all men mortal but himself, he goes to work and takes his
chance.   Seamen, too, are far more unprotected than other
men, and this is especially so in the case of overloading (so
great a cause of disaster), for their articles are signed before-
hand, they have no voice in the matter of loading ; and if
they refuse to sail for any cause, they can be, as they have
been, and as they are, sent to gaol for periods of three
weeks to three months ; and men have, to my own knowledge, gone to sea and to death in spite of tearful entreaties
of wife and sister, driven by this cause alone, owing to the
almost invincible repugnance of respectable men (the men
I have in my mind were engineers) to the contamination,
the degradation, of a common gaol.

No ; what with the general insensibility to danger to
themselves, who have lived so long in this way of life, and
come safe through so many perils—and what with the
shrinking from the charge of cowardice and the repugnance
to gaol of even those whose apprehensions are aroused, I
am satisfied we cannot with any reason (as we certainly have
no right to) look for remedy to the unaided seaman.

Ship-owners.—Cannot we then look to the ship-owner, to
his sense of justice, to his self-interest, to put a stop to this
deplorable state of things ?

We shall be better able to answer that question if we
consider the process by which it has come to pass that,
whereas in the early part of this century every ship was the
subject of the most anxious care on the part of her owner
or owners, who neglected no known means of providing for
her safety, and when from age or decay she could no longer
be sent to sea with safety, she was broken up ; it is now the
case (as to a considerable portion of our mercantile marine)
that necessary repairs are so systematically neglected that it
can be said with truth, as it is said by the Committee of the
National Life-Boat Institution, that " such is the notoriously
ill-found and unseaworthy manner in which vessels are sent

on their voyages, that in every gale—even if it be of a moderate character only—it becomes a certainty that numbers of them will be destroyed." Well may they add—" It is overwhelming to contemplate the loss of life from these, in too many instances *avoidable*, wrecks." Before insurance was adopted, every ship was, after every long voyage, most carefully overhauled. If she was found to need repairs, those repairs were carefully executed; if her cordage or rigging was getting tender, it was replaced with rigging new and strong—nothing was neglected to insure her safety; her return home was watched for with the utmost solicitude and anxiety. Her safe return was an occasion of great rejoicing, in which the whole family of the ship-owner participated. Presents and various indulgences signalised the happy time. So much so was this the case, that presents were promised in anticipation of her return, and at last it settled into a household word, and such and such a thing was to be done, and such and such a present was promised, all to be redeemed " when my ship lands."

Gradually, however, as insurance came into general use, this great care was relaxed a little. Trade was too good and busy for the customary overhauling, and it was put off till after the next voyage. Then perhaps it was done, or perhaps the same considerations pleaded for yet further delay. These temptations to delay received a powerful (though perhaps unconscious) support, in the reflection that now that the ship was insured the owner's property was safe in any event.

At all events, it must be admitted that the owner was no longer prompted by that great anxiety about the safety of his property which formerly weighed upon his mind, with such good results that there was absolutely no necessity to legislate in a sense requiring him to watch over the safety of his vessel, and to execute all needed repairs promptly, regularly, and efficiently.

Or, another set of reasons came into operation. Trade was so bad, and profits so small, that really he could hardly afford to be continually watching for an opportunity of spending money, and really the ship looked very well, and we may very safely defer the next examination until after another trip. For a time old habits prevailed to keep up a tolerably decent state of things; but, slowly and surely, the habits and practice which were born of anxiety for the safety of his property, and fear of loss, changed when that anxiety ceased to exist, and when the loss could no longer overtake him.

So well was this understood to be the case, that after some years of the existence of Lloyd's as an institution for insurance, the insurance people themselves instituted another society or committee, henceforward to exist alongside the older society, and now by outsiders confounded with it. The object of this society (Lloyd's Register Committee) was to collect information as to the state of ships, their age, state of repair, &c. For the guidance of the underwriters, this committee adopted the plan of classifying the ships, and eventually the present elaborate and most useful system was the result. But more of this further on.

I have shown how the modern practice of insurance operated in relaxing the vigilance formerly exercised in keeping up the repairs of a ship. I will now show its effects in relaxing the good old rule of loading, viz.—that for every foot depth of hold (measuring from the under-side of the main-deck to the keel) 3 inches should be left above the water line, summarised as " 3 inches of side to the foot of hold."

When you consider how small an addition to the fair load of a ship will augment the profits of a trip 25, and even 50, per cent., you will easily see how great was the temptation, especially in settled weather, to add the extra weight.

When freights run low, the margin for profit over expenses is small; it may take nine-tenths of the cargo to pay the costs; an addition, then, of only 10 per cent. to the weight of the cargo will double the profit, and 20 per cent., which will still leave the ship in trim difficult to find fault with, will treble the earnings; and when we consider the enormous advantage this gave to the reckless, and the temptation to even those who disapproved of the practice to follow it in self-defence, it is really wonderful to me that the practice should now be, as it undoubtedly is, confined to only a section of the trade.

When this temptation was held in check by the fear of losing the ship, no harm was done—prudence prevailed to prevent too great a risk being run; but when that fear was withdrawn, it is not to be wondered at that the caution bred of it disappeared also, and little by little a system of over-loading has grown up amongst the needy and reckless section of ship-owners, which, as you have seen, the Board of Trade charges with a large portion of our entire losses at sea. Sometimes, too, it was not merely greed that did this; the managing clerk of the wharves to and from which the ship works has much ado to get freight sometimes, and a good deal of canvassing among merchants. The freight comes in answer; what is he to do? There is more than can be considered a safe load. To leave part over for the next trip is to give offence to the sender, and to neutralise the results of much solicitation. The weather is good; the trip not a very long one: *it must go.* The captain perhaps remonstrates; but the managing clerk presses, perhaps says, as I have known them to say, "Oh, captain, you're getting timid as you get into years." And eventually it goes—goes safely, too; for, remember, it is only a few of the over-loaded ships that are overtaken with the fate they tempt, and this success is urged then on future occasions as an unanswerable reply to any further remonstrance by the captain, and what was once the exception becomes the rule. A captain once complained to me that the clerk had said to him, "Oh, Captain ——, you are getting afraid!" "Afraid?" he said, "I wished he was out with me some nights that I'm out—one night of it would turn his hair white with fear."

When we consider the force and the continued pressure of these two temptations—neglect of repair and overloading—I think we have great cause for thankfulness that affairs are no worse, for it is well known in seaport towns that the great majority of our ship-owners do keep up repairs, and do not overload. It is only a few who do these things, and ship-owners, as a body, repudiate these practices, and have repeatedly memorialized the Board of Trade in favour of the adoption of a maximum load-line on the side of the ship, below which she should not be allowed to be loaded, and a compulsory survey by its officers of all unclassed ships. To put the case shortly,—before insurance was practised, legislation was not needed; a new state of things has now arisen, which Parliament has not yet given attention to.

Clearly, then, we can no more look to ship-owners to remedy these evils (they having, as a class, done what they could), than we can to the seamen, nor to the underwriters, —and are, therefore, as clearly driven to this conclusion: That it is the duty of society generally to interfere, through the State, to extend to seamen the same degree of care as is bestowed on so many classes of our fellow-subjects. I say society, instead of Government, because no Government can well move in the matter until public opinion requires it. Society means the individuals comprising it—therefore it is on you, who read these lines, that this great, this life-giving duty now devolves—you personally—not Parliament only, not Government merely, but *you*.

I will suppose, and God grant, for the sake of our poor brothers on the deep, that you are convinced; and, being convinced, are willing to render what aid you can in remedying this evil; and will then, with you, now consider its extent, its more particular sources, and the remedy. But, before I go to this, I want just to say a word about insurance. Is insurance a bad thing, since it has destroyed that anxious care for his own property in a few ship-owners, which formerly tended so greatly to preserve the lives of the seamen? I don't think it is; it is an unmixed good for all the other ship-owners, and, by giving greater security to the trade, has greatly tended to increase our mercantile marine, to the great advantage of the nation; and with regard to the minority, a very simple legislative enactment would have prevented these temptations from becoming so great

as to involve dangerous results. In Holland the law prohibits a ship-owner, under heavy penalties, from insuring a
ship for more than two-thirds of her value—value determined
not by owner, but by a public officer. He, the ship-owner,
thus enjoys all the legitimate advantages of security, and
still remains under the wholesome dread of loss so necessary
to ensure all proper precautions being taken to secure the
safety of the men.

Precedents.—But, you may ask, shall we not, if we interfere in this matter, be establishing an inconvenient,precedent,
laying down a new and untried principle which may subsequently be very embarrassing, and possibly lead to undesir-
able results? No, we shall not ; we shall simply be acting
in accordance with precedent. We shall be only doing for
those who need it most (and who, but for the fact that politically they are the weakest class of all our fellow-subjects,
would long since have had it done for them), what has
already been done for nearly all classes ashore.

Only last session, another and most beneficial measure
was added by Parliament to several preceding ones, the
object of which was to benefit, and diminish the risk to, the
coal miner, the ironstone getter, and indeed all classes of
miners. These measures contain many and very minute
regulations respecting the modes in which mines must be
sunk and opened. You must not work a coal mine with
less than two shafts, the additional one being simply to give
another chance of escape to the men in case of accident ;
and, what is more to the purpose, a large staff of scientific
men, paid by the State, is appointed to INSPECT these mines,
—men whose attention is constantly occupied in considering the causes of accidents, and the precautions best adapted
to prevent their recurrence.

All operatives in factories—men, women, and children—
work under conditions imposed by the law ; and these, too,
have a large and efficient staff of inspectors, who see that
the provisions of the law are properly complied with, that
the revolving machinery is properly fenced off, &c., and
these inspectors are paid by the State.

By the Act passed August 15, 1867, all the following
classes of workmen ashore are cared for : those who work
in—

> Mills,
> Forges,
> Foundries,
> Premises in which steam and water-power are em-
>   ployed,
> Manufactories of machinery,
> Paper manufactories,
> Glass manufactories,
> Tobacco manufactories,
> Letterpress printing and
> Bookbinding manufactories.

This Act, amongst other things, prohibits the taking of
meals in certain factories, enacts the use of a fan in others,
and that grinding-stones shall be fixed in accordance with
certain conditions in others.   The persons charged with
seeing to the due observance of the Acts are appointed and
paid by the State.   The Act 30 and 31 Vic., c. 103, even
regulates the hours in which alone children, young persons,
and women shall work, and enacts the employment of certain
mechanical means with a view to preserving their health;
and imposes heavy penalties on any person who shall in any
way impede the inspector charged with the duty of seeing
the provisions of the Act carried out.

30 & 31 Vic., c. 141, regulates the relations of masters
and servants in certain cases, to the end that the latter may
be better protected.   And since I have been in Parliament
an Act has been passed abolishing imprisonment for breach
of contract by a workman, and substituting civil action as a
remedy.   Yet to this day if a seaman refuses to go to sea in
a ship after signing articles, he is sent handcuffed and to
prison for three months, even though he may have been
induced to sign articles under a promise that the ship should
be repaired before she was sent to sea, which promise was
afterwards disregarded.

We have inspectors of food ashore who seize and condemn meat unfit for food, and prosecute those who send it to market. No such inspection is employed with regard to seamen's provisions, and hence all unmarketable food is reserved for them; and I am assured by a dockmaster in one of our largest ports, that though respectable ship-owners do not ship bad provisions, there is a minority who ship meat which would be condemned in any market in England.

If a manufacturer or merchant ashore fails, the claims for wages of his workmen are a first charge upon his estate, and must be paid in full. No such provision applies to seamen, and I know of many cases of the greatest hardships which are the result. In one case known to me the crew of a ship returned from a very long voyage (eighteen months), when the ship and cargo were seized by the mortgagee, and the seamen, who were entitled to some £50 each as wages, were sent adrift without anything.

In the autumn of 1870 the Privy Council issued an order that no sheep should be imported into English ports after the 30th of September or before the 1st of April unless sheltered from the weather on board. On March 25, 1871, seven men, for refusing to proceed to sea in a ship in which their sleeping bunks were, as was proved, " very wet, so much so that they were obliged to sleep in their oilskin clothing," were brought ashore, handcuffed by the Margate police, and chained together on the jetty, and were followed by a great number of people, " many deprecating the manner in which they were secured," and the report adds that they were committed to the county gaol for twelve weeks' hard labour:

> " Rule Britannia, Britannia rule the waves,
> For Britons never, never, never, &c., &c., &c."

The last instance I shall cite of the care of Parliament for the safety of the subject's life ashore is the Building Act, passed August 14, 1855.

This Act specifies with great detail the minimum strength of timber which shall be employed for supporting floors, proportioning it to the length of bearing, &c. It also prescribes the thickness of the walls, distinguishing dwelling-houses from warehouses in both cases, and varying the thickness of the walls as the materials used vary, making a distinction between stone and brick, and between rubble stone and hewn stone, and having regard also to the height of the walls; whilst anybody may build a ship of what he likes, and may just put in as much or as little, as sound or as rotten timber, as he pleases—there is none to interfere.

Parliament, too, looks after the safety of sight-seers, and when some person questioned the safety of an orchestra at the Agricultural Hall some time ago, the matter was heard before Mr. Barker, a metropolitan magistrate, who forthwith made an order for strengthening timber to be added, and Mr. Moseley, the district surveyor, was charged to see the work done. Again, on the occasion of the day of thanks-giving for the restoration to health of the Prince of Wales, the attention of the Home Secretary was called to the probable insecurity of some of the private erections made for persons viewing the procession, and the matter was attended to at once, the Metropolitan Board of Works being charged with the duty, in aid of the efficient discharge of which duty the police were ordered to assist.

I show here a couple of openings in the Building Act to illustrate the very scrupulous care with which Parliament watches over the safety of life ashore :—

[18° & 19° VICTORIÆ, Cap. 122.

Metropolitan Buildings (Schedules).

FIRST SCHEDULE.

PRELIMINARY.

Structure of Buildings.   1. Every Building shall be enclosed with Walls constructed of Brick, Stone, or other hard and incombustible Substances, and the Foundations shall rest on the solid Ground, or upon Concrete or upon other solid Substructure.

2. Every Wall constructed of Brick, Stone, or other similar Substances shall be properly bonded and solidly put together with Mortar or Cement, and no Part of such Wall shall overhang any Part underneath it, and all Return Walls shall be properly bonded together. *Construction of Walls of Brick, Stone, &c.*

3. The Thickness of every Stone Wall in which the Beds of the Masonry are not laid horizontally shall be One Third greater than the Thickness prescribed for Stone Walls in the Rules herein-after contained. *Extra thickness of certain Stone Walls.*

4. The Thickness of every Wall as herein-after determined shall be the minimum Thickness. *Thickness of Walls.*

5. The Height of every topmost Story shall be measured from the Level of its Floor up to the under Side of the Tie of the Roof, or up to Half the vertical Height of the Rafters, when the Roof has no Tie ; and the Height of every other Story shall be the clear Height of such Story exclusive of the Thickness of the Floor. *Height of Story.*

6. The Height of every External and Party Wall shall be measured from the Base of the Wall to the Level of the Top of the topmost Story. *Height of External and Party Walls.*

7. Walls are deemed to be divided into distinct Lengths by Return Walls, and the Length of every Wall is measured from the Centre of one Return Wall to the Centre of another; provided that such Return Walls are External, Party, or Cross Walls of the Thickness herein-after required, and bonded into the Walls so deemed to be divided. *Length of Walls.*

8. The Projection of the Bottom of the Footing of every Wall, on each Side of the Wall, shall be at least equal to One Half of the Thickness of the Wall at its Base; and the Diminution of the Footing of every Wall shall be formed in regular Offsets, and the Height from the Bottom of such Footing to the Base of the Wall shall be at the least equal to One Half of the Thickness of the Wall at its Base. *Footings of Walls.*

PART I.

RULES FOR THE WALLS OF DWELLING HOUSES.

1. The External and Party Walls of Dwelling Houses shall be made throughout the different Stories of the Thickness shown in the following Table, arranged according to the Heights and Lengths of the Walls, and calculated for Walls up to One Hundred Feet in Height, and supposed to be built of Bricks not less than Eight and a Half Inches and not more than Nine and a Half Inches in Length, the Heights of the Stories being subject to the Condition herein-after given. *Thickness of Walls of Dwelling Houses.*

2. Table.

I.	II.	III.	IV.
Height up to 100 Feet.	Length up to 45 Feet. Two Stories, 21½ Inches. Three Stories, 17½ Inches. Remainder, 13 Inches.	Length up to 80 Feet. Two Stories, 26 Inches. Two Stories, 21½ Inches. Two Stories, 17½ Inches. Remainder, 13 Inches.	Length unlimited. One Story, 30 Inches. Two Stories, 26 Inches. Two Stories, 21½ Inches. Two Stories, 17½ Inches. Remainder, 13 Inches.
Height up to 90 Feet.	Length up to 45 Feet. Two Stories, 21½ Inches. Two Stories, 17½ Inches. Remainder, 13 Inches.	Length up to 70 Feet. One Story, 26 Inches. Two Stories, 21½ Inches. Two Stories, 17½ Inches. Remainder, 13 Inches.	Length unlimited. One Story, 30 Inches. Two Stories, 26 Inches. One Story, 21½ Inches. Two Stories, 17½ Inches. Remainder, 13 Inches.
Height up to 80 Feet.	Length up to 40 Feet. One Story, 21½ Inches. Two Stories, 17½ Inches. Remainder, 13 Inches.	Length up to 60 Feet. Two Stories, 21½ Inches. Two Stories, 17½ Inches. Remainder, 13 Inches.	Length unlimited. One Story, 26 Inches. Two Stories, 21½ Inches. Two Stories, 17½ Inches. Remainder, 13 Inches.
Height up to 70 Feet.	Length up to 40 Feet. Two Stories, 17½ Inches. Remainder, 13 Inches.	Length up to 55 Feet. One Story, 21½ Inches. Two Stories, 17½ Inches. Remainder, 13 Inches.	Length unlimited. One Story, 26 Inches. Two Stories, 21½ Inches. One Story, 17½ Inches. Remainder, 13 Inches.
Height up to 60 Feet.	Length up to 30 Feet. One Story, 17½ Inches. Remainder, 13 Inches.	Length up to 50 Feet. Two Stories, 17½ Inches. Remainder, 13 Inches.	Length unlimited. One Story, 21½ Inches. Two Stories, 17½ Inches. Remainder, 13 Inches.
Height up to 50 Feet.	Length up to 30 Feet. Wall below the topmost Story, 13 Inches. Topmost Story, 8½ Inches. Remainder, 8½ Inches.	Length up to 45 Feet. One Story, 17½ Inches. Rest of Wall below Topmost Story, 13 Inches. Topmost Story, 8½ Inches. Remainder, 8½ Inches.	Length unlimited. One Story, 21½ Inches. One Story, 17½ Inches. Remainder, 13 Inches.
Height up to 40 Feet.	Length up to 35 Feet. Wall below Two Topmost Stories, 13 Inches. Two Topmost Stories, 8½ Inches. Remainder, 8½ Inches.	Length unlimited. One Story, 17½ Inches. Rest of Wall below Topmost Story, 13 Inches. Topmost Story, 8½ Inches. Remainder, 8½ Inches.	
Height up to 30 Feet.	Length up to 35 Feet. Wall below Two Topmost Stories, 13 Inches. Two Topmost Stories, 8½ Inches. Remainder, 8½ Inches.	Length unlimited. Wall below Topmost Story, 13 Inches. Topmost Story, 8½ Inches. Remainder, 8½ Inches.	
Height up to 25 Feet.	Length up to 30 Feet. From Base to Top of Wall, 8½ Inches.	Length unlimited. Wall below topmost Story, 13 Inches. Topmost Story, 8½ Inches. Remainder, 8½ Inches.	

3. In using the above Table the Height of the Wall is Explanation of to be reckoned on the First vertical Column on the Left Tables. Hand of the Table, and the Length of the Wall on the corresponding horizontal Column. The Thickness of the Wall in each Story is given in Inches, and begins with the Wall from the Base upwards.

4. If any External or Party Wall, measured from Qualification in Centre to Centre, is not more than Twenty-Five Feet case of certain distant from any other External or Party Wall to which Walls. it is tied by the Beams of any Floor or Floors, other than the Ground Floor or the Floor of any Story formed in the Roof, the Length of such Wall is not to be taken into consideration, and the Thickness of the Wall will be found in the Second vertical Column in the above Table.

5. If any Story exceeds in Height Sixteen Times the Condition in Thickness prescribed for the Walls of such Story in the respect of above Table, the Thickness of each External and Party Stories exceed- Wall throughout such Story shall be increased to One ing a certain Sixteenth Part of the Height of the Story; but any such Height. additional Thickness may be confined to Piers properly distributed, of which the collective Widths amount to One Fourth Part of the Length of the Wall.

6. No Story enclosed with Walls less than Thirteen Restriction in Inches in Thickness shall be more than Ten Feet in case of certain Height. Stories.

7. The Thickness of any Wall of a Dwelling House, if Thickness of built of Materials other than such Bricks as aforesaid, Walls built of shall be deemed to be sufficient if made of the Thickness Materials other required by the above Tables, or of such less Thickness than such as may be approved by the Metropolitan Board, with this Bricks as Exception, that in the Case of Walls built of Stone in aforesaid. which the Beds of the Masonry are not laid horizontally no Diminution shall be allowed in the Thickness required by the foregoing Rules for such last-mentioned Walls.

8. All Buildings, except Public Buildings, and such Rule as to Buildings as are herein-after defined to be Buildings of Buildings not the Warehouse Class, shall, as respects the Thickness of being Public their Walls, be subject to the Rules given for Dwelling Buildings or Houses. Buildings of the Warehouse Class.

PART II.

RULES FOR THE WALLS OF BUILDINGS OF THE WARE-HOUSE CLASS.

1. The Warehouse Class shall comprise all Ware- Definition of houses, Manufactories, Breweries, and Distilleries. Warehouse Class.

E

Thickness at‘ 2. The External and Party Walls of Buildings of the
Base.   Warehouse Class shall at the Base be made of the Thickness shown in the following Table, calculated for Walls
up to One Hundred Feet in Height, and supposed to be
built of Bricks not less than Eight and a Half Inches and
not more than Nine and a Half Inches in Length.

3. TABLE.

'I.	II.	III.	IV.
Height up to 100 Feet.	Length up to 55 Feet. Base, 26 Inches.	Length up to 70 Feet. Base, 30 Inches.	Length unlimited. Base, 34 Inches.
Height up to 90 Feet.	Length up to 60 Feet. Base, 26 Inches.	Length up to 70 Feet. Base, 30 Inches.	Length unlimited. Base, 34 Inches.
Height up to 80 Feet.	Length up to 45 Feet. Base, 21½ Inches.	Length up to 60 Feet. Base, 26 Inches.	Length unlimited. Base, 30 Inches.
Height up to 70 Feet.	Length up to 30 Feet. Base, 17½ Inches.	Length up to 45 Feet. Base, 21½ Inches.	Length unlimited. Base, 26 Inches.
Height up to 60 Feet.	Length up to 35 Feet. Base, 17¼ Inches.	Length up to 50 Feet. Base, 21½ Inches.	Length unlimited. Base, 26 Inches.
Height up to 50 Feet.	Length up to 40 Feet. Base, 17¼ Inches.	Length up to 70 Feet. Base, 21½ Inches.	Length unlimited. Base, 26 Inches.
Height up to 40 Feet.	Length up to 30 Feet. Base, 13 Inches.	Length up to 60 Feet. Base, 17¼ Inches.	Length unlimited. Base, 21½ Inches.
Height up to 30 Feet.	Length up to 45 Feet. Base, 13 Inches.	Length unlimited. Base, 17½ Inches.	
Height up to 25 Feet.	Length unlimited. Base, 13 Inches.		

Explanation of   4. The above Table is to be used in the same manner
Table.   as the Table previously given for the Walls of Dwelling
Houses, and is subject to the same Qualifications and
Conditions respecting Walls not more than Twenty-five
Feet distant from each other.

5. The Thickness of the Walls of Buildings of the Warehouse Class at the Top, and for Sixteen Feet below the Top, shall be Thirteen Inches ; and the intermediate Parts of the Wall between the Base and such Sixteen Feet below the Top shall be built solid throughout the Space between straight Lines drawn on each Side of the Wall, and joining the Thickness at the Base to the Thickness at Sixteen Feet below the Top as above determined ; nevertheless in Walls not exceeding Thirty Feet in Height the Walls of the topmost Story may be Eight Inches and a Half thick. *[Thickness at Top of Walls and through intermediate Space.]*

6. If in any Story of a Building of the Warehouse Class the Thickness of the Wall, as determined by the Rules herein-before given, is less than One Fourteenth Part of the Height of such Story, the Thickness of the Wall shall be increased to One Fourteenth Part of the Height of the Story; but any such additional Thickness may be confined to Piers properly distributed, of which the collective Widths amount to One Fourth Part of the Length of the Wall. *[Condition n respect of Stories exceeding a certain Height.]*

7. The Thickness of any Wall of a Building of the Warehouse Class, if built of Materials other than such Bricks as aforesaid, shall be deemed to be sufficient if made the Thickness required by the above Tables, or of such less Thickness as may be approved by the Metropolitan Board, with this Exception, that in the Case of Walls built of Stone in which the Beds of the Masonry are not laid horizontally no Diminution shall be allowed in the Thickness required by the foregoing Rules for such last-mentioned Walls.] *[Thickness of Walls built of Materials other than such Bricks as aforesaid.]*

No means are neglected by Parliament to provide for the safety of life ashore; and yet, as I said before, you may build a ship in any way you please—you may use timber utterly unfit, you may use it in quantity utterly inadequate, but no one has any authority whatever to interfere with you.

You may even buy an old ship 250 tons burden by auction for £50, sold to be broken up because extremely old and rotten; she had had a narrow escape on her last voyage, and had suffered so severely that she was quite unfit to go to sea again without more being spent in repairs upon her than she would be worth when done.

Instead of breaking up this old ship, bought for 4*s.* per ton (the cost of a new ship being £10 to £14 per ton), as was expected, you may give her a coat of paint—she is too rotten for caulking—and, to the dismay of her late owners, you may prepare to send her to sea. You may be remonstrated with twice, in the strongest terms, against doing so, even to being told that if you persist, and the men are lost, you deserve to be tried for manslaughter.

You may then engage men in another port, and they, having signed articles without seeing the ship, you may send them to the port where the ship lies, in the custody of a runner. You may then (after re-christening the ship, which ought not to be allowed), if you have managed to insure her heavily, load her until her main-deck is within two feet of the water amidships, and send her to sea. Nobody can prevent you. Nay, more, if the men become restive you may arrest them, without a magistrate's warrant, and take them to prison, and the magistrates (who have no choice, they have not to make but only to administer the law) will commit them to prison for twelve weeks with hard labour; or, better still for you, you may send for a policeman on board to overawe the mutineers, and induce them to do their duty! And then, if the ship is lost with all hands, you will gain a large sum of money, and you will be asked no questions, as no inquiry even will ever be held over the unfortunate men, unless (which has only happened once, I think) some member of the House asks for inquiry.

The river policeman who in one case threatened with imprisonment a refractory crew, and urged them to do their duty!! told me afterwards (when they were all drowned) that he and his colleague at the river-side station had spoken to each other about the ship being dreadfully overloaded, as she passed their station on the river, before he went on board to urge duty! and that he then, when he saw me, "rued badly that he hadn't locked 'em up, without talk, as then they wouldn't have been drowned."

The fact is, that before insurance became general, there was no need of legislation; and now a new state of things has arisen, which the law has not yet provided for.

But besides the ample powers given in the Act of 1855, as to the materials to be used in building a house or warehouse, and which the quotation shows fully, Parliament also conferred power on the surveyors to give notice to the owner of any house, dwelling-house, warehouse, factory, or other building, if he found it to be in an unsatisfactory state, and order that such and such a wall must be pulled down and rebuilt, and in cases where he deemed the whole structure unsafe, he might order it forthwith to be pulled down; and that this power is used vigorously and well I have had ample means of knowing, for I some few years ago bought a great number of houses, near the Elephant and Castle, in London, for the purpose of pulling down some of them. The others were not wanted, and were allowed to remain; and it is with respect to these I speak. In a comparatively short time after the purchase I received several notices, some that such a gable was out of the perpendicular, others that a front wall was in a similar condition: in two other cases the notice was to pull down altogether, all of which was done. I show three of the notices :—

[Notice of Works.

Form No. 6.   *Registered No. 541.*

1287

ꟿꜳetropolitan Woard of ꟿꟿorks.

Metropolitan Building Act, 1869.

DANGEROUS STRUCTURES.

TO the Owner and Occupier of the Structure known as No. 6, *Arch Street (flank wall)*, in the Parish of *St. Mary, Newington*, and County of *Surrey*.

The METROPOLITAN BOARD OF WORKS, acting in the execution of the Metropolitan Building Act, 1869, having received information that the above-named Structure is in a dangerous state, and having required a survey thereof to be made by a competent Surveyor, and having had his opinion certified to them to the effect that the said Structure is in a dangerous state : DO, by this writing, give you Notice, and require you forthwith *to take down the said flank wall where bulged or defective.*

Metropolitan Board of Works,   GEORGE VULLIAMY,
    Spring Gardens,   *Superintending Architect.*
   19th day of January, 1870.

N.B. This Notice does not supersede the necessity of your giving the usual Notice to the District Surveyor two days before commencing the work of rebuilding, &c., agreeably to 38 Sect. 18 & 19 Vict. Cap. 122, Part I.

Such Fee in respect of the Survey of the above Structure as may be directed by the Metropolitan Board of Works, or other expenses (if any) incurred by the said Board, is to be paid by the Owner (as defined by the Act) of the said Structure to the Cashier of the Board, at the Offices of the Board, Spring Gardens. Such Fee is distinct from any fees payable to the District Surveyor.   ]

[Notice of Works.
    Form No. 6.   *Registered No.* 542.

1288

Metropolitan Board of Works.

Metropolitan Building Act, 1869.

DANGEROUS STRUCTURES.

TO the Owner and Occupier of the Structure known as No. 7, *Meadow Row (flank wall), New Kent Road,* in the Parish of *St. Mary, Newington,* and County of *Surrey.*

The METROPOLITAN BOARD OF WORKS, acting in the execution of the Metropolitan Building Act, 1869, having received information that the above-named Structure is in a dangerous state, and having required a survey thereof to be made by a competent Surveyor, and having had his opinion certified to them to the effect that the said Structure is in a dangerous state : DO, by this writing, give you Notice, and require you forthwith, *to take down the said flank wall (late party wall).*

Metropolitan Board of Works,   GEORGE VULLIAMY,
    Spring Gardens,   *Superintending Architect.*
   19th day of January, 1870.

N.B. This Notice does not supersede the necessity of your giving the usual Notice to the District Surveyor two days before commencing the work of rebuilding, &c., agreeably to 38 Sect. 18 & 19 Vict. Cap. 122, Part 1.

Such Fee in respect of the Survey of the above Structure as may be directed by the Metropolitan Board of Works, or other expenses (if any) incurred by the said Board, is to be paid by the Owner (as de- fined by the Act) of the said Structure to the Cashier of the Board, at the Offices of the Board, Spring Gardens. Such Fee is distinct from any fees payable to the District Surveyor.   ]

[Notice of Works.

Form No. 6.   *Registered No.* 311.

Metropolitan Board of Works.

Metropolitan Building Act, 1869.

DANGEROUS STRUCTURES.

TO the Owner and Occupier of the Structure known as *a house at the corner of Meadow Row and Rockingham Street,* in the Parish of *St. Mary, Newington,* and County of *Surrey.*

The METROPOLITAN BOARD OF WORKS, acting in the execution of the Metropolitan Building Act, 1869, having received information that the above-named Structure is in a dangerous state, and having required a survey thereof to be made by a competent Sur- veyor, and having had his opinion certified to them to the effect that the said Structure is in a dangerous state : DO, by this writing, give you Notice, and require you forthwith, *to remove the said building.*

Metropolitan Board of Works,   ,GEORGE VULLIAMY,
    Spring Gardens,   *Superintending Architect.*
; *1st day of January,* 1870.

N.B. This Notice does not supersede the necessity of your giving the usual Notice to the District Surveyor two days before commencing the work of rebuilding, &c., agreeably to 38 Sect. 18 & 19 Vict. Cap. 122, Part 1.

Such Fee in respect of the Survey of the above Structure as may be directed by the Metropolitan Board of Works, or other expenses (if any) incurred by the said Board, is to be paid by the Owner (as de- fined by the Act) of the said Structure to the Cashier of the Board, at the Offices of the Board, Spring Gardens. Such Fee is distinct from any fees payable to the District Surveyor.   ]

I don't complain of this, I think it a good thing that unsafe structures should be made secure, and when needful pulled down; but is it not wonderful that while all this power should be given (and wisely given), and vigorously and beneficially exercised, in the case of buildings when the safety of a few is concerned, and those not in imminent danger, that there should, as was stated in evidence recently, not be any legal power whatever to prevent a vessel going to sea, no matter what condition she was in ?*

A still stronger precedent, however, may be cited. It is this :—That whilst it is all true which I have stated of merchant ships, every word of it, it is not the case with passenger ships. They are, and have been for years, surveyed by officers appointed by the Board of Trade at the cost of the Government. They are so surveyed twice in every year. What I want, and what I greatly wonder the working classes have not long ago demanded, is that the same measures of safety be employed when members of their order are concerned, as are deemed needful, and employed, in the case of those who are above them.

Clearly there is no lack of precedent.

What, then, is the extent of the evil you are now asked to aid in remedying ? This is soon shown. I show you in the Frontispiece a lithograph of the wreck chart published by the Board of Trade for the year ending December, 1871.

Here I give the number of lives lost on the English coast within ten miles for the last eleven years :—

Lives lost in 1861	.	884	Lives lost in 1867	.	1,333
,, 1862	.	690	,, 1868	.	824
,, 1863	.	620	,, 1869	.	933
,, 1864	.	516	,, 1870	.	774
,, 1865	.	698	,, 1871	.	626
,, 1866	.	896			

* This was literally true last year, and is substantially true now, the qualification being, that in the Act passed last year on the withdrawal of my bill, a sailor is empowered to demand a survey, and if the vessel is found unseaworthy she may be detained; but the sailor, if a surveyor report that in his opinion the ship is seaworthy, is to pay all the costs! And the captain is especially empowered to stop them out of his wages! What a mockery, what trifling is this!

You will see that there is a considerable reduction in the figures for the past two years. Whether this is owing to exceptional weather or not, I am not competent to say, or whether it is owing in part to the attention called to the subject in Parliament by the bill I then introduced, and the vigorous denunciations of prevalent practices which issued from all parts of the House, and which that year resulted in the measure introduced by Government on the withdrawal of mine, I cannot say.

Suppose the former case, better weather accounts for it. In that case the weather of former years may recur.

Suppose the latter cause operated, the attention of Parliament effected the change. Some will say, "How satisfactory!" "Let us go on as we are now—improving." I say, No. If the diminution is owing to the mere expression of opinion only in Parliament, what may be anticipated from legislative enactment?*

Now, then, what are the more particular sources of all this loss of life?

In dealing with the more definite sources of preventible shipwreck, I will glance briefly, in the first instance, to the less important ones, and then take overloading and neglect of repairs.

Amongst causes of less frequent disaster at sea, the practice of sending a ship on her voyage with *too small a number of men* to manage the vessel properly or efficiently in bad weather is one. There may be men enough to handle her in fair weather; but when bad weather comes on, especially if it comes abruptly, they are too few for the work, and many valuable lives are sometimes lost owing to this cause.

I know one ship-owner who has so high an opinion of the efficiency of an able-bodied English sailor, that he occasionally

---

* It must be borne in mind that losses in the open sea are not included in the figures I have given. There is besides these an enormous loss of life at sea; in the present month (January, 1873) no less than twelve grain-laden steamers are reported missing.

sends his ships to sea with a surprisingly small number of
them on board. On an occasion I was informed of, he
sent a full-rigged ship to a port in the Baltic with eleven
men only on board. Now, a full-rigged ship has three masts,
and they all carry square sails, as they are called to dis-
tinguish them from the fore-and-aft canvas carried by a
barque on her mizen-mast, and by brigantines and schooners.

When it is considered that to trim any one sail—that is,
to place it at a different angle to the wind which is blowing
—many ropes have to be manipulated, and that until *all*
the sails are so adjusted the ship is in a sort of transitional
position, what chance, I ask, is there that eleven men could
handle the ship with effect, either to tack, wear, or shorten
sail ?

I know also of another case, where a steamship of 1,500
tons was sent from Liverpool on a voyage to the East with
only eight deck hands aboard. Here, too, the number of
men was fearfully inadequate to meet probable contingencies.

Now, I do not recommend at present the adoption of
any inelastic rule to regulate numbers of hands to tonnage ;
because it would doubtless be found that a crew which
would be barely sufficient for one vessel might be more than
enough for another vessel of similar tonnage, but which was
better equipped in other respects, or of different rig. All
that seems to me needful in this case is that all masters and
captains should in future make a return of the number of
men and boys under eighteen on board at the time of sailing, together with the tonnage of their vessels. By this
means very valuable information would be accumulated
of the numbers usually employed by careful ship-owners,
and probably, in cases like those I have quoted, a quiet
note from the Board of Trade would be found sufficient to
prevent a recurrence of such reprehensible recklessness.

Bad stowage is another source of loss sometimes. By
bad stowage is meant that the cargo, perhaps a mixed one,
is so put on board that the centre of gravity of the entire
bulk—ship and cargo—is too much or too little below the

meta-centre, or centre of displacement round which a vessel moves in rolling.

If the ship is loaded with dead weight—say iron or ore—if care is not taken to put something between it and the floor of the hold, the centre of gravity will be too low down in the ship—too far below the centre of displacement. In that case she would be what is technically called too "stiff" —her sides would offer too stubborn a resistance to the shock of a wave, and the ship would be greatly strained, and after heeling over a little under a blow, the weight of cargo being too low in her, she would recover her perpendicular with such an abruptness, with such a shock, as would tend to almost shake her masts out of her.

If the centre of gravity of the load were higher up, she would yield to the blow, and heel over until it passed, and would then roll easily back again, without subjecting either frame or masts to any violent strain.

If, however, the centre of the weight were too high up, that is, too near the centre of displacement, she would roll too easily, and consequently too much; she would now be called too "crank" for safety, because in extreme instances she would roll over altogether, and founder. This result is often occasioned by the desperately dangerous practice of deck-loading, a practice which ought to be altogether prohibited from January 1 to March 31, and from October 1 to December 31 in each year, and only permitted in summer by special license, as the cargo so loaded not only tends to make her top-heavy (too crank), but greatly impedes the seamen in handling the ship.

In shipping mixed cargoes, then, care and judgment are required to so arrange the weight that she shall be neither too "stiff" nor too "crank."

This is frequently difficult to manage, for it is not as though all the freight destined to form her cargo were alongside at the outset of loading—then it would be easy enough; but the wrong goods come first, it may be, and must be stowed as they come, and although it is easy to ascertain her state after loading, it is not so easy so to load such a ship as that she shall be just as one could desire.

There is another cause of disaster which I must include here, as it is one which is responsible for very many of our most heavy losses—foundering at sea—I mean *inadequate engine-power.* Many, very many of our cargo-carrying steamers are far too weak in engine-power ; they have just sufficient power to make, when heavily loaded, headway across the water, and when rough weather occurs, they are entirely helpless. As this, however, is one of the matters which a commission only can fully ascertain and deal with, I content myself with enumerating it merely.

Over-insurance is another of the sometimes sources of danger; and that this arises, and can only arise, from down-right wickedness, no one can fail to perceive. A man has property in risk ; he wishes to insure himself against that risk—so long as he is fully indemnified by underwriters of responsibility, the less money he can obtain this security for the better.

Yet we hear of instances continually where a man induces the underwriter, by falsehood and fraud, to take some hundreds of pounds of his money per annum from him more than is necessary to fully insure him against the utmost possible amount of his loss in the event of shipwreck. Now, a man in business who lays out money, does so with the expectation of getting it back, and with a profit ; but in this case he cannot get a profit—he cannot even get his bare outlay again, or any equivalent for it, except in the event which it is an insult to any one's judgment and common sense to ask them to believe he did not actually take measures to bring about—that is, the wreck of his ship.

Why, even reading the newspapers only, sufficient comes to light at intervals to show what results from the right to insure or over-insure to any amount.

A case came before the Lord Mayor of London, some time ago, where a man, having been detected, was accused of endeavouring to compass the loss of his ship, and he confessed that, although he had insured his vessel for £1,000, it had only cost him £300 !

Another case was heard before the magistrates at North Shields of a similar nature. The owner was charged with trying to bring about the loss of his ship. In this case it was shown (and he indeed confessed) that, although he did not think the vessel would sell for £400, he had effected an insurance upon her for £800.

One more case must suffice, and then I shall proceed to the next topic. It should be premised that when a merchant vessel is lost at sea, even with all hands, no inquiry at all is ever made into the circumstances. In this instance, however, on the motion of a member in the House, an inquiry (the first of the kind) was instituted.

I will place before you that part of the evidence of the owner himself which related to insurance, and then show you a paper given me by the gentleman whose name it bears.

" Mr. ——, the witness in question, was then cross-examined by Mr. O'Dowd, and said that he was joint owner of the —— with Mr. ——, and the ship was bought by them of its late owners for £7,500.

" They paid down £1,000 in signing the contract, and £1,500 more before the ship proceeded to sea."

Now read this :—

June 10, 1870.

" The —— was insured this day for twelve months, was valued at £13,000 ! the premium of insurance being eight guineas per cent. !

      (Signed)   " W. M. F——G."

Here you see the owners make a declaration that the ship was worth £13,000, they having only given £7,500, and they actually succeeded in insuring her for £10,000, so securing £2,500 in excess of their real loss when the ship sank, as she shortly afterwards did, with every soul on board; twenty good, decent, respectable men, as I can personally testify, at least as to several of them, went down in her.

I urge, therefore, that in no case should a ship-owner be allowed to insure his ship for more than two-thirds of its value, properly ascertained. A certain sum per ton measurement should only be allowed, and this should vary with her class, her age, and other considerations. There would be no difficulty in tabulating a scale by the Board of Trade, and you will be of that opinion after seeing the careful tables respecting buildings I have shown in an earlier part of this letter.

I know it will be represented by some that it would be a hardship to prevent a man from fully securing himself against loss. My answer is, "You ask us to entrust twenty, twenty-five, or thirty precious lives on board your ship. The state of that ship depends solely on you. You only have authority to care for her safety ; we must, therefore, take hostages from you, that when you take twenty or more human lives on board, no reasonable means of safety shall be neglected, and if you are too poor to run this risk of one-third, you have no business to be a ship-owner at all, considering how many lives are placed in your hands."

Defective construction next claims a few words.

There is, I fear, great reason to think that ships are occasionally lost from the very imperfect manner in which some of them are built; in some cases I think you will see that something much worse ought to be said. I don't say the cases are many ; still, they exist, and we have done nothing to prevent it.

The first time I introduced a bill to prevent overloading, I alluded (mentioning no names) to the case of one ship-owner who, trading to the West Indies for sugar (a good voyage, deep water and plenty of sea-room all the way), had, out of a fleet of twenty-one vessels, lost no less than ten of them in less than three years !

After I had concluded my speech in moving the second

reading, a member accosted me in the lobby and said, "Mr. Plimsoll, you were mistaken in that statement of yours."—"What statement?" I answered.—"Oh! that where you said a ship-owner had lost ten ships in less than three years from overloading."—"I mentioned no names," I said.—"No; but I know who you meant; it was Mr. ——, of ——. He is one of my constituents, and a very respectable man indeed. It is not his fault, it is the fault of the man who built his ships, for one of them was surveyed in London, and was found to be put together with devils. Mr. —— knew nothing about it, I assure you." — "Devils?" I said.—"Yes."—"I don't know what you mean."—"Oh, devils are sham bolts, you know; that is, when they ought to be copper, the head and about an inch of the shaft are of copper, and the rest is iron."

I have since found there are other and different sham bolts used, where merely a bolt-head without any shaft at all is driven in, and only as many real bolts used as will keep the timbers in their places.

Now these bolts are used to go through the outside planking, the upright timber rib, and the inner planking (ceiling) of a ship, and through the vertical or drooping part of a piece of timber or iron called a knee, on the upper part of which the deck-beams rest, and to which the deck-beams are also bolted from above. These bolts are therefore from thirteen to eighteen inches in length.

Well, I did not see at the time why an iron bolt should not do as well as a copper one; it only looked like cheating the buyer of the ship. But some time after, in the course of my inquiries, I was shown some specimens of iron taken out of a ship, which were eaten away in the strangest manner. Strong plates looked much as though they had been cakes of glue, and boiling water had been poured upon them from a kettle. The iron was wholly eaten away in many large places; the indented edges of the remainder were thin as a sixpence; and, strangest of all, much of what was left was neither more nor less than plumbago!—simply blacklead ! !—which you could write with on paper, and break quite easily with your hand.

The conversion is the result of chemical action. The sugar, combined with the acid of the timber, and assisted by the bilgewater, changes iron into—blacklead !

Now, indeed, the iron devils, which a member of the House of Commons told me in excuse for his constituent, the owner, had been put into ships by the builder, seemed another and very different thing.

What is to happen to such a ship when the acid has done its work, its strength turned to rottenness? What is to hinder her, the heads of the bolts eaten off, when labouring in a heavy sea, from opening her sides, from falling abroad, and with destruction so sudden that there is no time even to get out the boats? This letter, which refers to this case, and which came into my possession shortly after, gives an awful, I might say a lurid reply.

[(COPY.)

    To ——, London.   *April*, 1870.

DEAR SIR,

    I beg to acknowledge receipt of your letter of the 12th inst.

    I have seen Captain —— upon the subject of your letter, and am informed by him that from what he has seen of Mr. ——'s vessels, he considers that, with the exception of some iron ships lately built at —— and ——, they are all of an inferior class, badly built by —— of ——. They are constantly under weigh, without examination of any kind, either of hull, sails, spars, or rigging—that is, they arrive with cargoes of sugar, are discharged, and sent away again laden with coals and iron, without receiving even necessary repairs, within a few days.

    Captain —— can only judge from outward appearance, not being allowed by Mr. —— to go on board.

    Mr. ——, of the —— Underwriters' Association, entirely confirms the above, and informs me that —— underwriters will not insure either vessels or cargoes, in consequence of their being badly built and ill-found, except in special cases, where the risk is good. Insurances are therefore effected in London, where they are not so well known.

    It is generally believed that Mr. —— and Mr. —— had some private arrangement between them in the building of the vessels. Mr. —— does not bear a good character as a builder.

    The fleet numbered in 1866-67, 21 vessels; in 1867-68, 17 vessels; and at the present time 21 vessels.

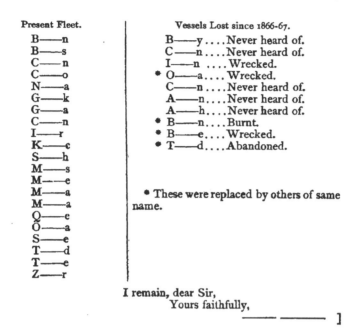

Present Fleet.	Vessels Lost since 1866-67.
B——n	B——y....Never heard of.
B——s	C——n....Never heard of.
C——n	I——n ....Wrecked.
C——o	* O——a....Wrecked.
N——a	C——n ....Never heard of.
G——k	A——n....Never heard of.
G——a	A——h....Never heard of.
C——n	* B——n....Burnt.
I——r	* B——e....Wrecked.
K——c	* T——d....Abandoned.
S——h	
M——s	
M——e	
M——a	* These were replaced by others of same
M——a	name.
Q——e	
O——a	
S——e	
T——d	
T——e	
Z——r	

I remain, dear Sir,
　　　Yours faithfully,
　　　　　—— ——]

Ten ships lost in three years! Five—one, two, three, four, *five!!*—so utterly that not a soul on board escaped to tell the tale! What horror is there in those three brief words,—" Never heard of ———" " Never heard of ———." Fathers, husbands, brothers, sons, all sacrificed to greed of gain, sent to their long account in a moment!

I am compelled to suppress the indignant horror this case excites, or I could not go on with my task; but how I should like that William Overend, Q.C., who wrenched the guilty knowledge out of Broadhead and Allen in Sheffield so inflexibly, had Mr. ———, the owner, and Mr. ———, the builder, under examination. How I should like to hear him demand of the owner the cost of each ship, and the sum for which each was insured;— to hear him demand of the builder how many of these devils were put into these ships. But I must not lose sight of my proper object in indignation. It is to save life, not to ruin reputations,—to preserve the homes of the poor from desolation, not to send disgrace into the homes of the rich. In a word, it is to reform a system, and not to seek a punishment of individuals, however richly merited, that I write to you.

The fault after all is ours. We had no right, knowing what human nature is, to leave such temptations, such powers, without safeguard or check.

To proceed, however. There are not only the dangers arising from faulty construction, but a new danger has recently arisen—arisen in this way. About twelve or more years ago, it was found that by having steamers made very much longer than was usual, very little, if anything, was added to the cost of working a vessel, whilst the additional space being all available for cargo (instead of being in great part occupied by machinery and fuel), double the quantity of cargo could be taken aboard, and without doubling the length of the ship. When iron steamers were first built, they were constructed five and sometimes six times as long as they were broad, and seven breadths in length was considered extraordinary.

Some years afterwards it was determined to build them longer, and gradually seven and eight breadths were taken, and then nine, and nine and a half breadths were taken as the measure of length, and these were found to carry exactly double the cargo of the others, and at the same speed, and very little more expense—no more, if they were carefully kept clean outside the hull.

A firm I could name went faster than all others in thus extending the length, for it was found that a ship which had been built seven breadths long, on having two and a half breadths more added to her length, carried twice as much as she could before ; and so gradually steamers were built longer, until ten and ten and a half breadths is now no uncommon length, and there are ships I can name now which are sixteen times longer than their depth—that is, from the top of the main-deck beams to the keel.

Last week, the third week in December, 1872, there was an account of the loss of a large steamer and a great number of lives (thirty), which was more than seventeen times as long as she was deep! The depth is (*cæteris paribus*) the measure of her strength to resist a vertical strain, as the breadth of beam is the measure of her strength to resist a side blow.

It would be more than I am able to say, lacking the special knowledge to enable me to form an opinion, that vessels cannot be constructed strongly enough even of these dimensions; but many shipbuilders are of opinion that we have exceeded the limits of safety.

But whilst I leave this an open question, there can be no manner of doubt but that a ship originally constructed of a much shorter length would have to be lengthened, if lengthened she must be, with very great and most careful precautions.

Now what is the case? Of course, it was not to be thought of, that the owners of the longer ships should be left in quiet possession of the enormously greater profit these longer ships made for them, by the owners of shorter ones, and the shorter ones were rapidly cut in two, and lengthened amidships; when this was done under proper supervision there was perhaps nothing much to complain of, but as there is no law on the subject, great numbers of them were lengthened in such a manner as to make their foundering at sea only a question of time. I will give one instance. The steam-ship ———— came into the possession of a very young man, without any knowledge of shipbuilding, and he desired to lengthen her fifty feet. He was strongly urged not to do so, as she would not be seaworthy. He was headstrong and insisted. Then he was urged to strengthen her by additional bulkheads, extra knees, and doubling several of the rows of plates outside. He again refused, and as no one could interfere, he had fifty feet put into her amidships, on the same scantling as the rest, nothing more; and she is now leaking like a basket, and I have added her name to my list of ships that I expect to founder.

I may add that one ship of that list has foundered this month (January, 1873), with an unusually large number of men, who were all lost; and as she did not carry passengers, no inquiry will ever be made, of course.

Now that young man can send the crew of that ship to prison if they, after engaging, refuse to sail in her; but they are not likely to refuse, for how are poor men to judge whether a newly-altered ship is seaworthy or not? And they very likely suppose that having been done recently she is all right—it will probably never occur to their minds that the English Government (so careful of the subject's life ashore, and even of their comfort) are so almost incredibly indifferent to the lives of sailors that, as a well qualified witness recently testified, " There is no legal power whatever to prevent a ship from going to sea, no matter what condition she is in ; " and that there is absolutely no restriction, no rules whatever, imposed on any one who chooses to build a ship ; he may do it just how he likes.

That young man may also send by the action of the Libel Law a good-hearted and most estimable gentleman to gaol for a long period if he venture to criticise his conduct too plainly, and therefore I refer to the case in general terms at the express request of my informant. A gentleman deservedly held in high public estimation was recently sentenced to a long term of imprisonment for libel, at the suit of a person of whose doings I shall have something to say if you help me to induce the Government to consent to the ·issue of a Royal Commission. I will content myself by saying here that there are gentlemen of high character in Cardiff, Newcastle, Greenock, Port-Glasgow (and the neighbourhood), London, Sunderland, Hull, Liverpool, and other places, who are longing for the opportunity of telling a Royal Commission what they know, but whose lips are now sealed by the terrible Law of Libel, and when that Commission (if granted by the Government) reports, they will disclose a state of things wholly disgraceful, shameful, and afflicting.

As it is extremely desirable that my statements should be vouched by higher authority than mine, and as the matter is one of such transcendent importance, I make this public appeal to the Right Hon. G. J. Goschen, First Lord of the Admiralty, as to whether I have not correctly described the position of underwriters in this matter; to Sir James Elphinstone, M.P. for Portsmouth, as to what he thinks of sending a spar-decked ship so loaded with iron that her main-deck was two feet ten inches under water, into the extreme east of the Baltic in November, and what he thinks of eleven men for a full-rigged ship; to J. D'Aguilar Samuda, Esq., M.P., and to Mr. Laird, M.P., as to whether it is not the fact that there are scores of vessels afloat and many steamers building, of such material, such dimensions, and such scantling, that no sane man, who understood these things, would trust his life in; and to any lawyer, as to whether I have not correctly described the law of the matter. I appeal to all these to state at their early convenience in the *Times* whether or no my statements are correct.

Now one can scarcely think it possible to lengthen a steamer considerably, however well it might be done, and still to have her as strong as if she had originally been built of the greater length, for in that case the naval architect would have adapted all the parts in their proper proportions to the greater length.

But still if steamers were lengthened carefully, and under proper supervision, no doubt they might still be good seaboats. Many were lengthened with all the care that could be wished, but as no ship-owner is under any rules or restrictions whatever, many were simply lengthened with materials and dimensions like those in the original structure, and were consequently much weaker than when originally designed. This, too, has been a source of greater loss of life than is generally supposed.

I know of one steam-ship which the owners desired to

lengthen ; they consulted a naval architect on the matter. He surveyed the ship, and reported that in his judgment she might be safely lengthened, if an additional iron bulk-head was put into her, and four pairs of additional knees, and if four rows or streaks of her outside plating were doubled across the added portion, such doubling to be continued over the severed portions nearly to her bows and stern.

Well, the owners begrudged the cost of this, and as there is no superior authority whatever, they disregarded his advice, and lengthened her without adding the bulkhead ; with only two pairs of additional knees, and instead of doubling four rows of plates outside nearly from stem to stern, they only doubled two, and only carried the doubling a few feet fore and aft beyond the added portion. The naval architect consulted told me she might, if lucky, go many voyages in safety, but that she was greatly weaker than before, and that she would fare badly, and would pro-bably be lost, in weather which, had she been properly lengthened, she could easily have pulled through, and that if she struck on a rock at any time she would break up like earthenware, and give no time for boats to be got out or anything else.

Only on Monday, December 2nd, 1872, I read an account of the loss of a large steamer, which stated that she had struck on a rock, broken in two, and gone down with all on board, as there was no time to get out the boats.

Now (but I speak this with deference to higher authority) it seems to me that no steamer, properly constructed of good iron or steel, would break in two like this ; at all events, I well remember the stem of an iron steamer (built in Sweden) being shown in the Great Exhibition of 1862, which steamer had struck on a rock with such force that her stem was, so to speak, crushed up and backwards in three folds, showing the tremendous force with which she had struck ; yet she did not even spring a leak, and when the bows were afterwards cut away to be replaced, the portion cut away was sent to the Great Exhibition to show how good the iron was.

I also remember seeing a steamer which rested loaded on the sill of a dock about midships ; her keel and keelson were bent upwards, and her mainmast lifted two feet out of her, yet she sustained no further damage, and was unloaded and the injured parts replaced, and she is now a good ship.

On one occasion I was myself on board a large passenger steamer from Ireland, which struck on the back of the Isle of Wight in a fog, and I shall not readily forget the horrible grating of her keel and the sudden stoppage which woke me up ; but though she remained a fixture for twelve hours, and could only be got off by lightening her of a great part of her cargo, and then only by the aid of two steamers and her own engines, she had sustained very little damage, showing she was a good strong ship.

The fact is, there is a good deal of cheap, bad work done in iron ship-building, by persons, too, whose names I can furnish at a proper opportunity.

But all these sources of occasional loss require carefully to be considered by competent men possessing special knowledge, and are such that I cannot ask you to pronounce upon them as to what remedies shall be applied. Excepting in so far as this, I think you are capable of forming an opinion upon the homicidal practice of over-insurance, and you can safely and with propriety say that no ship-owner ought to be allowed to insure for more than two-thirds of the value of his ship. You can also express a good opinion as to the propriety of requiring a return from all captains of the number of men on board on leaving port.

But if it requires special and professional knowledge to deal with the causes of disaster I have been examining, there is no man of intelligence in the kingdom who is unable to pronounce emphatically and decisively upon the two remaining causes of preventible wreck ; and, happily for the sailors, they are the admitted sources of more than half our annual loss of life. I say happily, because these causes admit of immediate remedy. The Board of Trade say in their report that " if the figures be examined, it will be found that about half of the total loss on the coast is to be attributed to over-loaded and unseaworthy vessels of the collier class. For the nine years ending in 1871 this loss is rather more than half." Now consider, with the information I have given you of the care of Government in other directions, do you not feel justified in asserting emphatically that no vessel needing repairs should be allowed to go to sea until those repairs were properly executed ? do you not feel equally able to say that no vessel should be allowed to be dangerously overloaded ?

I repeat, Can any valid reason be given against the quali-fication of any landsman to say, that ships needing repair shall be repaired, and that ships shall not be over-loaded ?

I might well rest the case as to *overloading* upon the state-ment of the Board of Trade, that more than half our losses for nine years (six years before 1868, and three since) were owing to unseaworthy and overloaded ships ; but I will give you one or two cases which came within my own knowledge :—

There was one ship-owner whose name was often men-tioned to me in the course of the years 1869 and 1870. During my inquiries in the north and east, I heard his name wherever I went as that of a ship-owner who was notorious for the practice of overloading and for a reckless disregard of human life. I therefore made inquiry as to the ships belonging to him which had been lost, with the number of lives lost in each case, and the reply I received I will show you. It is incomplete, you see ; but sufficient is shown to demonstrate the necessity of Government interference.

[(COPY.)
                                        20th February, 1871.
MY DEAR SIR,

 Annexed I forward a more complete list of Mr. ——'s losses, together with the number of lives sacrificed. I think I shall be able to send you a further list of sailing vessels, but a melancholy list of 105 lives lost will be almost enough evidence to produce against him.

Date.	Ships Lost.	Lives Lost.
1867.........s.s.	C——th	—
1868........	A——s	—
,, ...	V——e	29
,, ...	F——e	10
,.	V——r	—
1869........	L——e	28
,, ...	P——n	—
,, ...	C——u	22
....	H——r	16
....	M——y	—
....	A——r	Not known.
....	L——s	,,

I am, my dear Sir,
Very truly yours,

Samuel Plimsoll, Esq., M.P., House of Commons.   ]

It is really awful to contemplate the loss of precious human life from the operations of this one man alone.

I don't suppose he has lost any since; for I threatened him to his face that I would bring the matter before the House of Commons, and it was pitiable to see the abject terror of the man. However, I will write to-night (December 9, '72) to my informant, and will insert his reply when it reaches me.—I now have it (December 20). This man has not lost a single seaman's life since !

Another case came to my knowledge. It was this :—

I must premise by saying that no prudent ship-owner will dispatch ships to the ports of the Baltic later than the end of September. The season then closes, and the lights are removed, to prevent their being carried away by the ice.

Mr. James Hall, of Newcastle-on-Tyne, had a large ship (1,500 tons) waiting for freight in the Jarrow Dock, and he was offered 30s. per ton to carry a cargo of railroad iron into the east of the Baltic. It was the middle of September; the rate was high; the ship was empty. It was, as he said, very tempting. So he sent for the captain of the ship, and asked him if he durst venture into the Baltic then. The captain said to him, " For God's sake don't send us into the

Baltic at this time of the year, sir. You might as well send us all to the bottom of the sea at once." Well, Mr. Hall declined the offer; but five weeks later the same offer was accepted by another ship-owner, and he proceeded to load one of his ships, and this was how he loaded her. She was a spar-decked ship. Now a spar-decked ship is to a flush-decked ship what a box-cart with side-boards is to a box-cart without them. When it is desired to make a spar-deck, half the ribs of the ship which go from the keel up and within the sides—that is to say, every alternate rib—is carried above the main or flush-deck upwards some seven feet, and another deck is constructed over the main-deck at that height. This is to enable the ship to throw off the seas, which break over the ship better, and if the cargo consists of light goods, affords more stowage.

Now, in consideration of the greater safety a spar-deck thus gives, she may be immersed much lower than a flush-decked ship, always counting from the main-deck, which is under the spar-deck : *i.e.* her main-deck, when she is loaded, may be much nearer the level of the water than if her main-deck had no spar-deck above it to enable her to throw off the seas. And whereas by Lloyd's rule three inches of every foot depth of hold (from main-deck to keel) ought to be above the water-line, if flush-decked, one and a half inches of the side of the ship below the main-deck is deemed sufficient in the case of a spar-decked ship.

Thus, it will be seen, in both cases must the line of the main-deck be above the water-line, the only difference in the two cases being how much.

Now as to cargo. Goods more than 40 cubic feet of which weigh a ton are called measurement cargo ; if they are so light that 80 or 85 cubic feet don't weigh a ton, they are still called and charged for as a ton. Goods of which 35 feet weigh a ton are called dead-weight. Now 5 cubic feet of iron weigh a ton, so that this is the heaviest dead-weight they carry, and, from the weight pressing on so small a space, it is the most dangerous cargo a ship can carry.

The ship I refer to was 872 tons register, and she was loaded with 1,591 tons !

Take another test. She was 17 feet deep in her hold; from top of keelson to bottom of keel 1 foot 6 inches; in all 18 feet 6 inches. According to Lloyd's and the Government rule she ought to have had her main-deck at least 2 feet 3¾ inches out of water, which, added to the height of the spar-deck, 7 feet, would give the height of her spar-deck out of water as 9 feet 3¾ inches; instead of her main-deck being above the water-line 2 feet 3¾ inches, *it was actually 2 feet 10 inches below the level of the water*, and her spar-deck was only 4 feet 2 inches above the water-line, instead of 9 feet 3¾ inches.

And this vessel, so loaded, was sent off to the Baltic in November, or five weeks later than the same freight had been refused by Mr. James Hall, of Newcastle-upon-Tyne, on the ground that it was too late in the season to send a ship without imminent peril to the lives of the seamen !

Of course she was lost—foundered about eighteen miles from the English coast (east); but fortunately her crew were saved by a fishing-boat.

She was insured, of course, and after what I have before said, you will not wonder that the underwriters paid the claim, no one of them having an interest large enough to make it worth while to engage in an expensive lawsuit. And this ship-owner had the hardihood to say to me, " The underwriters have paid, and is not that proof that all was right ? "

I said to him, " You know what that defence is worth ; " and then he talked about the terrific weather that the ship had had; but I had provided myself with a copy of the protest, which contradicts itself, for instance—6 a.m., wind blowing a perfect hurricane; 10 a.m., foretopsail had to be taken in ! What sort of a perfect hurricane could it have been when they could carry topsails? Then the protest says, the log-book was lost with the ship, and yet gives the following times in the protest's narrative—1.45 p.m., 8 p.m.,

9.20 p.m., 10.30 p.m., 6 a.m., 9 a.m., noon, 8 p.m., 3 a.m., 6 a.m., 7 a.m., 8 a.m., 9 a.m., 10 a.m., 4.30 a.m., 7 a.m., 8 a.m., 4 p.m., 10.15 a.m., noon, 4 p.m., 5.25 p.m., 6 a.m.

Is it not obvious that the narrative is got.up, or that the statement that the log-book went down with the ship is wholly untrue?

How is it, also, that the mate did not sign the protest?

Of the ships also which had left the same port on the same day, and of those which sailed for three days before and three days after, not one (they had been looked up) had met with the slightest accident or bad weather.

But it is childish to seek any other reason for the ship foundering than her excessive load and the season of the year. This man, I may say, before I dismiss him for the present, actually assured a public meeting that the charges of overloading were grossly exaggerated, for that *he* himself had assisted the officers of the Board of Trade to go over all the alleged cases of overloading from the north-eastern ports, and had satisfied them that these charges were all groundless, except in one case! Poor Board of Trade!

Now, How is overloading to be ascertained?

There are several rules which find favour with ship-builders. The oldest is that known as Lloyd's rule, viz. three inches of side (sometimes called freeboard) for every foot depth of hold. This is also the invariable rule of loading enforced by Government when they charter ships for conveyance of stores, &c.; but some contend, and with reason, that if a ship is unusually broad of beam, less than three inches will be safe.

Again, an iron ship may, in the opinion of Liverpool authorities, be loaded more deeply than this with safety, when her hold is not more than twenty-one feet deep; while, if she is twenty-three feet deep and upwards, they would give her more freeboard than Lloyd's scale demands.

Other authorities contend that the true measure should be three-tenths of the total displacement of the ship as side above water. The Liverpool scale for wooden ships also allows rather deeper loading for vessels under seventeen feet depth of hold, and requires much lighter loading than that claimed by Lloyd's rule for vessels having holds deeper than twenty feet.

On occasion of one of my visits to a port in the north, I was met by a gentleman who knew what my errand there was likely to be, and he said, "Oh, Mr. Plimsoll, you should have been here yesterday; a vessel went down the river so deeply loaded, that everybody who saw her expects to hear of her being lost. She was loaded under the personal directions of her owner, and the Captain himself said to me, 'Isn't it shameful, sir, to send men with families to sea in a vessel loaded like that?' Poor fellow, it is much if ever he reaches port."

Mr. C—— B——k said, as he saw her, "That ship will never reach her destination."

Mr. J—— B—— said, "She did not look to be more than 12 or 14 inches out of the water."

Mr. J—— H——, a policeman, said to his colleague, "Dear me! how deep she is!"

Mr. W—— B—— said to a friend, standing by his side, "Dear me! this vessel appears very deep in the water."

Mr. J—— S—— said, "It strikes me she is dangerously deep."

The Captain called on his friend, Mr. J—— H——, who said he (the Captain) was greatly depressed in spirits. He told him (Mr. H——), "that he" (the Captain) "had measured her side loaded, and she was only 20 inches out of the water." He also asked his friend to look after his (the Captain's) wife. Mr. H—— gave him some rockets in case of the worst, and then they shook hands and parted.

J—— N—— and —— C——, two workmen, said to each other, "that they would not go in that ship if the owner would give them the ship." And J—— L——, another workman, said "he'd rather go to prison than go in that ship;" and lastly, two of the wives of two of the sailors at least begged the owner "not to send the vessel to sea so deep."

She was sent. The men were some of them threatened, and one at least had a promise of 10*s.* extra per month wages to induce him to go. As she steamed away, the police boat left her; the police had been aboard to overawe the men into going. As the police boat left her side, two of the men, deciding at the last moment that they would rather be taken to prison, hailed the police, and begged to be taken by them. The police said "they could not interfere," and the ship sailed. My friend was in great anxiety, and told me that if it came on to blow, the ship *could not* live.

It did blow a good half gale all the day after, Sunday— the ship sailed on Friday. I was looking seaward from the promontory on which the ruins of T—— Castle stand, with a heavy heart. The wind was not above force 7— nothing to hurt a well-found and properly loaded vessel. I had often been out in much worse weather, but then this vessel was not properly loaded (and her owner stood to gain over £2,000 clear if she went down, by over-insurance), and I knew that there were many others almost as unfit as she was to encounter rough weather—ships so rotten that if they struck they would go to pieces at once; ships so overloaded, that every sea would make a clean sweep over them, sending tons and tons of water into her hold every time, until the end came.

On Monday, we heard of a ship in distress having been seen; rockets had been sent up by her; it was feared she was lost. On Tuesday, a name-board of a boat was picked up, and this was all that was ever heard of her.

Mr. D——d was quite correct. On the Saturday he saw his wife reading the newspaper, and said to her, "Look out for the ——— in a day or two. I saw her go out of the river. She is sure to be lost." She was lost, and nearly twenty men returned home never more.

Mr. B—— and his brother told me that one day they saw a vessel leaving dock; she was so deep, that having a list upon her, the scuppers on the low side were half in the water and half out. (A list means she was so loaded as to have one side rather deeper down than the other; the scuppers are the holes in the bulwarks that let the water out which comes on deck from rain, from washing, and the seas breaking over her.) They heard a slight commotion on board, and a voice said to the Captain, "Larry's not on board, sir." He had run for it. Nothing could be done for lack of time to seek him, so they sailed without him. And these gentlemen heard the crew say, as the vessel slowly moved away from the dock gate, "Then Larry's the only man of us'll be alive in a week." That vessel was lost.

The *L*——, a large ship, was sailing on a long voyage from a port in Wales, with a cargo of coal. Mr. B—— called a friend's attention to her state. She was a good ship, but terribly deep in the water. Mr. B—— said, "Now, is it possible that that vessel *can* reach her destination unless the sea is as smooth as a mill-pond the whole way?"

The sea does not appear to have been as smooth as a mill-pond, for that ship was never heard of again, and twenty-eight of our poor, hard-working, brave fellow-subjects never more returned to gladden their poor wives and play with their children.

The *S*—— *B*——, a large ship, put to sea one day. She was so deep, that Mr. J—— M——l said to me as she went, "She was nothing but a coffin for the poor fellows on board of her." He watched and watched, fascinated almost by the deadly peril of the crew; and he did not watch for nothing—before he left his look-out to go home, he saw her go down.

Do you doubt these statements? Then, for God's sake —oh, for God's sake, help me to get a Royal Commission to inquire into their truth! Surely I don't ask too much, in asking *that*, for the sake of these poor brothers of ours, so shamefully neglected, so murderously treated.

The variation in these scales is urged as a reason why no

one scale should be adopted, but most dishonestly so, as
there is no difficulty. I would allow the ship-owner to
choose which he liked of all the scales, and load as deeply
as any of them would allow; or if he have more ships
than one, then any part of any rule for each of his ships. I
only want to prevent his being a rule to himself, and loading his vessel much, very much, deeper than any scale
allows or than any competent authority would sanction,
and if he is still dissatisfied, I would give him an appeal to
the Board of Trade.

You see no special knowledge is needed here, and you
who never saw a ship, or don't know a ship from a barque,
or a brig from a schooner or brigantine, you are just as able
to express an opinion, *and, better than that, you will on this
point.*

Let provision be made for painting on the ship's side
what the Newcastle Chamber of Commere calls the " maximum load-line," and that no ship under any circumstances
be allowed to leave port unless that line be distinctly
visible at or above the water-line; and let this fact be
ascertained and communicated to the Board of Trade by a
photograph of the vessel's side as she leaves the port or
dock. It will not cost more than a few shillings, and
would save a great deal of false swearing afterwards.

Now as to repairs.

How is the state of repair of a ship to be ascertained ? Just
as it is now in the case of ships carrying passengers, by a
surveyor appointed by the Board of Trade ; but instead of a
survey every six months, an annual survey would probably
be found sufficient.

On this point, too, I apprehend you now feel no difficulty
in forming an opinion, *and also of expressing your will.*

Before I go on to indicate the probable results of these
changes, there are two minor points to notice.

No re-christening of a ship should be allowed, under any
circumstances. It is a not infrequent thing to do to get rid
of an evil reputation, and sailors are sometimes led by this

into signing articles to go in a ship, which, had they known what I may call her real name, they would not have done. (I know of some cases myself.)

Underwriters, also, are thus sometimes cheated into insuring a villainous craft, which they would certainly not have done had the ship been offered for insurance in the name by which she was better known.

The case of the Deal boatmen, also, ought to have attention. They—and not sometimes, but often—are signalled for help by vessels in distress, and gallantly they go to her help in almost any weather ; but when they reach her, her condition may be different, or, fortified by the knowledge that help is at hand, the captain calls upon the crew for one more effort—for a little further struggle ; the men (encouraged, it may be, by the help at hand) respond, and they get out of their perilous position. In this event, the boatmen, who have perhaps rowed miles in a most dangerous sea, and often in the night, too, are sent empty away, if indeed they are not, as sometimes happens, laughed at. We don't treat a cabman even, in this way ; and provision should be made that, if signals of distress are used, at least the first boat that reaches the ship which signals should be remunerated, whether the services of the boatmen are required or not.

There is another source of much suffering to seamen which would cost but little to set right.

It is well known to those acquainted with seafaring topics, that a considerable number of seamen are shipped for long voyages, and almost altogether unprovided with proper clothing—many of them are put on board with nothing but what they have on; and in cases where the voyage is to cold latitudes much suffering is the consequence, men sometimes losing their toes from frost, and even when the consequences are not so serious their sufferings are very great.

I admit that their unprovided state is often (but not always) the result of their own improvidence, but if judg-

G

ment were laid to the line and righteousness to the plummet, which of us could stand? besides, Parliament has interfered to prevent Irish tenants from making bargains manifestly against their interests, and when it is considered how infinitesimal the additional cost to a ship's equipment would be, if a small supply of extra clothing were required to be carried on board, to be supplied on fair terms to the seamen in such cases, I cannot think any serious objection would be made to such a requirement when the acute and prolonged suffering it would obviate is considered.

These three points disposed of, I will now ask you to think of the enormous saving of life which would ensue from the prevention of overloading, and from the due execution of necessary repairs.

The Board of Trade's evidence must be again cited. They show conclusively that more than half our losses are owing to unseaworthy and overladen ships *of the collier class;* but there are other ships beside collier ships which are unseaworthy, and overloading is not a practice confined to colliers.

Compulsory survey, then, and prevention of overloading, applied to all merchant ships, would result in the saving of all those lives which are lost from these causes in the rest of the merchant navy.

No one unacquainted with the facts can have any idea what a total change would ensue at once from the prevention of overloading, but you can form some idea of it from the consideration of the following fact, showing how safe ships are when properly found, manned, and loaded. Mr. George Elliot, M.P., and his partners, have a fleet of steamers running between the Tyne and London continuously—the *Tanfield, James Joicey, Orwell, Newburn, New Pelton, Trevithick, Magna Charta, William Hunter, Berwick, Osworth, Carbon,* and others. These ships put into London from fifty to seventy cargoes of coal each per annum—the *Tanfield* having put sixty-eight, sixty-nine, and sixty-eight in three successive years. They are loaded and unloaded by machinery, and as they go and come more than once in each week, they are all *at least three-fourths of all the hours that come from year's end to year's end on the sea.* The voyage is a more dangerous one than an over-sea voyage, for as soon as they leave the Thames the sands and shoals and channels amongst which they pick their way begin. There are a whole crowd of dangerous shoals off the Essex coast alone to be avoided or steered between, as the case may be, as soon as the ships leave the Thames :—the Mouse Sand, the Long Sand, the Sunk, the Barrow, the Gunfleet, the Wallet, and the Kentish Knock Sands, all to be guarded against; the Cutler, the Cork, the Whiting, and the Shipwash Sands; the Corton Sand, the Newton, the Pakefield, and the Holm, off the Suffolk coast; the Cross, the Scroby, the Barber Sands; the Hasboro' Sand and the Sherringham Shoal, and the Ower and Leman, off the Norfolk coast. Look at any one of the wreck charts before referred to, and see what toll of our men's lives the Suffolk and the Norfolk coasts take. These sands are all under water even when the tide is ebb, but there is not water enough on them to float a ship, hence the losses when ill-found, overloaded, and under-manned ships get on them. Look at the next list of wrecks, and you will see that "she grounded on the Scroby Sand," or "she was lost on the Hasboro' Sand," or "the Sherring-ham Shoal," &c. Then there is the dangerous water enclosed by the Dudgeon, the Outer Dowsing, and the Spurn Head Lights; and higher up come the dangerous rocky coasts of Yorkshire and Durham. And all these have to be passed; but as there is no weather in these latitudes which is fairly responsible for the wreck of a single ship, except foggy weather, since no sound and well-found vessel, properly loaded and manned, is ever lost in them, all these ships of the truly honourable member, George Elliot, go and come in such absolute safety that during all the years from 1859, when the Jarrow Dock was first opened, until now, not one of them has been lost, nor even met with a casualty worth naming.

This is the case also with the fleets of many other ship-owners, for it cannot be said too often that nearly the whole of our loss is due to a comparatively small number of ship-owners tolerably well known in the trade.   The large majority do take reasonable precautions for securing the safety of their servants' lives.

Another instance will suffice to illustrate this position, that with reasonable care the dreadful losses we suffer would almost entirely disappear.   Mr. G. Reid writes me from—

" 19, Richmond Road, Bayswater, London,
"*February* 17, 1871.

*   *   *   *   *   *

" About the year 1860 the firm of Anthony Gibbs and Sons, Bishopsgate Street, London, took a contract from the Peruvian Government at Lima (Peru), to charter and load ships at the Chincha Islands with guano, and as many as between three and four hundred ships yearly left those islands for different parts of the world.   At first they were allowed to load and proceed to sea without either being inspected or surveyed before or after loading, and were permitted to load as deeply as the masters thought fit.*   The result of such neglect—losses and casualties very often occasioned.   Many ships foundered at sea, sometimes with all hands on board, others put back to the nearest port, in a leaky, disabled state, so much so that hardly three days would pass without hearing of some accident and loss, through the ships being allowed to overload and proceed to sea in an unseaworthy condition.   Mr. Stubbs, who was at the head of the house of Anthony Gibbs and Sons at Lima—he having to charter all the ships for loading guano—held a meeting, which passed a bye-law that for the future all ships, before being chartered by that firm, or allowed to load when chartered previously in England, should be surveyed by their surveyor before loading, and inspected after being loaded; afterwards a certificate being signed by the surveyor, stating the condi-

* Just as we do now in England.

tion and necessary repairs wanted—if any required—and sent in to the office; a copy given to the master of the ship, and in the same certificate the height of side was given that the ship was to finish loading with. As soon as the ship had been reported loaded, she was inspected, pumps well sounded, pumps sealed for twenty-four hours or less, side measured, and if all things found satisfactory, a certificate was given to that effect, and a copy given to the master of the ship, allowing him to proceed to sea, as soon as he had received his clearance from the custom-house, which he could not get until he had produced his certificate from the surveyor, stating the ship was in a fit and sound state to proceed to sea.

" Soon after the above rules were enforced a sudden and wonderful improvement took place, and during the four years I was surveyor afterwards *not one ship foundered at sea*, and only about two or three per cent. met with accidents ; and, to confirm what I have stated, you have only to apply to Mr. Stubbs, at the firm of Anthony Gibbs and Sons, London. That gentleman will be able to give very useful information on the subject, for I had the honour of being surveyor at Callao under him."

Do not these facts bear me out in saying that if we give proper care to the matter, our losses will almost entirely disappear ?

From a full consideration of the matter, from various opinions of practical men, gathered from time to time by me, I am of opinion that at least two-thirds of our total loss might be avoided, if not three-fourths ; for practical men of high-standing contend that no steam-ship well built and found and properly manned and loaded will founder at sea —they say that her doing so is her own condemnation !

See here how our task clears up before us, as we address ourselves with energy to its proper execution. It is as though God, in calling upon us to do our duty, were making the way plain and easy to us. I have enumerated and

examined several sources of loss,—no less than nine. Seven
of these I don't urge you to express yourself upon, on the
ground that they call for special knowledge in their treatment ; yet with only two on which you can with full confi-
dence give a verdict, these two rules of conduct only
adopted,—that ships needing repair shall be repaired, and
that ships shall not be overloaded,—we have this magnifi-
cent reward for prompt and decisive action, that no less
than two-thirds of the annual loss so much deplored will at
once become a thing of the past. It almost makes one's
heart leap to contemplate the prospect, that by the end of
1873 this fearful loss of life will be so grandly decreased.

Objections ! (of course there will be objections ; let us
examine them) :—

There will be the question of expense. Indeed, when I
introduced my bill the first time, a gentleman connected
with the Government went so far as to say it would cost
£500,000 a year. Well, suppose it did ; I, for one, deny
utterly that it would be any the less our duty to do it. But
would it cost £500,000 ?

To answer this question I must shortly describe the con-
stitution of Lloyd's. There are two bodies called "Lloyd's."
The older society is that of the underwriters, who undertake
the business of insurance, &c. From and in close connection with this arose Lloyd's Register Committee, in
1834. This Committee was formed to supply the underwriters with trustworthy information about ships, and they
undertook the survey of ships, which when surveyed they
classified, and of which they published a list, the first of
which was published in 1834. There was a list of some
sort before, 1819 is the earliest I can find. It was from the
outset intended that this Committee should be self-supporting, the price of the list and the fees charged for surveys
being expected to cover all their expenses. Thus there was
no necessity for any capital, nor for any proprietary, nor is
there any proprietary now. Their surveys, it was unexpect-
edly found, besides supplying information to the under-

writers, gave additional market value to ships, as capitalists ignorant of much relating to ships could now invest in ships with safety, as well as a person possessing sufficient tech-nical knowledge to value a ship himself. So, from surveying ships already built, their surveyors were asked to overlook the construction of ships in process of being built, for which one shilling per ton was charged. These ships are marked in the Register with a +, and these are very carefully sur-veyed three times during their construction.

First. When the frame is completed, the timbers dubbed (adzed) fair inside and outside, all ready for the planking and ceiling, but before the latter is put on.

Second. When the beams are put in, but before the decks are laid down, and with at least two streaks of the plank of the ceiling between the lower deck and the bilge unwrought, to admit of an examination of the inner surface of the planking of the bottom.

Third. When completed and before the planking is painted or otherwise covered. Ships so marked with a + stand much higher than others, they sell for more money, and they can be insured at lower rates.

The scale of fees settled at the outset, from the rapid extension of their operations, soon became much more than was wanted to pay their expenses, salaries of surveyors, &c. What was to be done? First, salaries were raised all round; and now their first-class surveyors all receive £800 per annum, and the lowest grade £200,—a scale of pay-ment so liberal that, as the very able and obliging secretary, Mr. Seyfang, told me, they were able to draw their young surveyors from the very best ranks of shipwrights reared in her Majesty's dockyards, where the payment is much smaller; but as this measure still left their income too high, they next reduced the fees. £10 10s. was reduced to £5 5s., and then £2 2s. was all that was charged for the half-time survey, and the charge for the annual survey was remitted altogether. Still the money came in faster than they could spend it, and one year I believe their surplus was not less than £18,000, and they now have a large sum accumulated, which, as they have no proprietary to divide it amongst, they literally don't know what to do with.

Now, I should never recommend the Government to do gratis for the careless and reckless ship-owner that for which the prudent and careful ship-owner pays! He ought to be charged, of course, fees not less in amount than those charged by Lloyd's. These fees would greatly exceed the expenses incurred by Government in the matter, and the surplus would go to the Chancellor of the Exchequer, like the surplus from the Post-office and from the Telegraph.

So much for the objection of expense.

But "*you would want an army of surveyors,*" objected the gentleman before referred to.

I again deny that even if this were so, it would absolve us from our plain duty. But how stands the case really? If their work was not only self-supporting, but brought in a surplus of revenue over expense, it matters not how many would be wanted, further than this, it might be feared whether sufficient surveyors could be found at short notice.

There is no need of apprehension on this score, however, for but few (seventeen) additional surveyors would be wanted. The proposal made by the Newcastle Chamber of Commerce in 1870, was that all *unclassed* ships should be surveyed (I shall explain unclassed further on).* But we must assert the principle of Government responsibility plainly and unmistakably, and this by enacting that all merchant vessels be surveyed by them, or under their authority, certain exceptions being scheduled in the Act, which schedule the Board of Trade should have power, from time to time, to add to or abridge.

Thus it would be readily admitted that the ships on Lloyd's List and the Book of the Liverpool Underwriters, already under very efficient supervision, should be excepted. The ships of the Cunard, the Peninsular and Oriental, and other lines carrying passengers, are already under survey,

* Page 109.

and would merely need that the load-line regulation should be applied. Not all of them would require even this, except for uniformity's sake.

The total number of ships registered in British ports at the beginning of the year was—

			Tonnage.
Sailing ships	.	22,510	.	4,374,511
Steam ships.	.	3,382	.	1,319,612
		25,892		5,694,123

Of this number of 25,892, there are 10,417 on Lloyd's Book for 1872, and there are 908 on the Book of the Liverpool Underwriters. These two totals, therefore, leave only 14,567 vessels to be dealt with, and this total is subject to further reduction by the number (of which I find no return) of passenger-carrying vessels already under survey by the Board of Trade.

During the first months of this change, too, all vessels built within five years might be left till the last, if necessary. These amount to 5,397, thus again reducing the number requiring immediate survey to 9,170, further reducible by the number of passenger-carrying vessels. But a still further reduction may be confidently reckoned on from the prospective action of the bill, if it be read a second time.

It is well known to, and it is vouched for by, a high authority I have seen in Sunderland, who says, " It is well known to myself and colleagues that there are some hundreds of ships sailing from the north-east ports which are utterly unfit to be trusted with human life. . . . . There has been no instance within my knowledge of a ship being broken up anywhere for many years. They insure them as long as they can, and when re-christening and all other dodges fail even with underwriters, then they form mutual insurance clubs, and go on until the ships fill and go down in some breeze, or strike and go to pieces." Have you reflected what the effect of a second reading of a bill which proposed to enact that vessels needing repair shall be repaired, would have upon these? It would result in great numbers being withdrawn and broken up, and in others being immediately taken up for repair.

The second reading would act upon all the rotten and worthless ships as the voice of the prophet of the Lord did upon the dry bones, when he cried, " Come from the four winds, O breath, and breathe upon these dry bones, that they may live." And our north-east sea-ports would become such a scene of wholesome and life-giving activity as has never yet been seen. This would reduce the number still further.

Now as Lloyd's have on their staff forty-one fully employed surveyors and seventeen partially employed, and as this staff surveys 10,417 ships, it is only a rule of three question as to how many additional surveyors would be required, even if no further use were made of the services of the surveyors already employed by the Board of Trade.

I have consulted many excellent authorities both in London and the north of England, and all agree that but few additional surveyors would be needed; my own estimate is seventeen. Mr. James Hall, of Newcastle, is sure less would be found sufficient after the first twelve months.

Further, I asked Mr. G. B. Seyfang, the secretary of Lloyd's Register Committee, and therefore the very best authority in England, if he thought there would be any difficulty about the matter. He fully discussed the matter with me, including all the points I have named, and his opinion, as nearly as I can remember his words, was :—" I do not think there would be much difficulty; we would gladly lend the Government all the help in our power, to the whole extent of our staff; we would even increase our staff, and probably the Liverpool Committee would give their assistance. Of course it would make everybody very busy, especially during the first twelve months, and it would be right that the surveyors should receive extra remuneration. Still, I have no doubt but that the thing could be done."

I have now dealt with the objection that an army of surveyors would be needed. The next objection I will notice (it was made in the House) is this :—

" That as Government would probably sanction the surveys of Lloyd's, &c., and the other Committee, it would amount to a recognition of private institutions."

Well, what of that ? we ought to be very glad that the necessities of commerce have already done so much of our work. Did not the Irish Land Act recognise what is called the Ulster custom, and enact that as it was just it should not be interfered with or displaced ? More, did it not enact that places where the custom did not already prevail might adopt it, and so remove themselves from the otherwise operation of the Act ?

Does an engineer having a road to make between two distant places, after levelling up ravines and tunnelling hills, refuse to recognise a fine stretch of level ground ?

But I have a still better answer to this objection than I had when I brought in my bill providing for the survey of unclassed ships, and for the prevention of overloading, for time has been on my side. Last year the Government wanted to make better provision for testing the strength of chain cables, and not having the means of doing the work itself, it expressly authorised the Board of Trade in the first schedule to the Act to adopt as their own work, work of this nature done under their authority by (*inter alia*) " The Committee of Lloyd's Register of British and Foreign Shipping," and " The Mersey Docks and Harbour Board," and some other bodies. So much for the dreaded principle of recognising private institutions. By the way, is it not passing strange that while the Government, in the view of diminishing loss of life, prescribe how many and what boats a ship must carry, how many and what lights she shall carry, and, as we have seen, takes pains that the ships' cables and anchors shall be adequate, it has not yet thought it necessary to see that the ships themselves are seaworthy ?

But, further says the mouthpiece of Government in replying to my speech :—

"If the Government were to interfere it would entirely destroy the ship-owner's responsibility." The answer to this is that (with one exception moved for by a private member) no inquiry or other investigation is ever made when a merchantman founders at sea, even with all hands, not carrying passengers. Mr. James Hall, of Newcastle, a large ship-owner, and an excellent authority on such subjects, said, in addressing the Associated Chambers of Commerce in London, in 1870 :—

"I know of no case where an inquiry has been held into the loss of any ship which may have foundered at sea, with all hands, passenger ships excepted."

*　　*　　*　　*　　*　　*

"I know of no case where a ship-owner has been held responsible for sending his ship to sea in an unseaworthy condition."

To talk, therefore, of destroying responsibility is nonsense. There is none, and therefore you can no more destroy it than you can steal a keyhole.

"But it will establish a dangerous precedent" if you interfere, said another member. The full evidence I have put before you regarding mines, factories, buildings, &c., &c., is a sufficient answer to this.

"But will you not encounter strong opposition from the ship-owners?" No—emphatically no! The Newcastle Chamber of Commerce appointed a sub-committee to report upon the provisions of the proposed Navigation Bill in 1869, and (*inter alia*) they reported that—"Your Committee strongly urge that there should be a periodical inspection of all sailing ships, unclassed at Lloyd's, or the Liverpool Underwriters' Association, and also of all unclassed steamships not carrying passengers ;" and subsequently the Chamber of Commerce of Newcastle-on-Tyne and Gateshead *petitioned Parliament* on the 15th March, 1870, in these terms—(I may here insert that they also memorialized the Board of Trade on the subject in November, 1869) :—

" That your Petitioners, as the commercial representatives of this town, are deeply interested in all matters relating to the Mercantile Marine.

"That your Petitioners would strongly urge that clauses should be inserted in the Bill providing for the periodical inspection (as at present provided for in the case of passenger-carrying ships) of all sailing ships unclassed at Lloyd's, or the Liverpool Underwriters' Association, and also of unclassed steamships not carrying passengers, and your Petitioners would point out that since provisions are contained in the Bill for the carrying of Boats, Lights, &c., it cannot be of less importance that the ship itself should be seaworthy.

" That your Petitioners respectfully draw attention to an abstract, presented to your Honourable House, of the returns made by the Board of Trade, of Wrecks, Casualties, and Collisions which occurred *on and near* the Coasts of the United Kingdom, from the 1st January to the 31st December, 1868. It is reported that—

" 'The number of ships lost or damaged in the 1,747 wrecks, casualties, and collisions reported in 1868, is 2,131 ; representing a register tonnage of 427,000 tons. The number of ships in 1868 is less than the number in 1867, by 382. In 1868 there were 131 wrecks and casualties to Smacks and other Fishing Vessels. Excluding these 131 Fishing Vessels, it will be seen that the number of vessels employed in the Carrying Trade that have suffered from wreck or casualty, during the year, is 2,000. If this number is again subdivided, it will be found that about half of it is represented by the unseaworthy, over-laden, or ill-found vessels of the Collier class, chiefly employed in the Coasting Trade. In the ten years ending 1868, 176 casualties happened to nearly new ships; 297 to ships from three to seven years old; 420 from seven to fourteen years old; 653 from fifteen to thirty years old; 267 from thirty to fifty years old; thirty-five between fifty and sixty years old; twenty-eight from sixty to seventy; nine from seventy to eighty; and eight from eighty to ninety years old. The age of 238 is unknown, but this year no casualties have been reported to vessels of known greater age than ninety years. . . . . . The state of rottenness and want of repair of some of the ships above twenty years old often calls for remark. Even at the age of twenty-five to thirty, it sometimes happens that a ship is so rotten as to fall to pieces immediately on touching the ground, without giving the crew the slightest chance of getting out their boats. The returns show that the number of lives lost in 1858 was 353, whereas in 1868 the number has been 824, being 507 less than in 1867. Of the 824 lives lost in 1868, 262 were lost in vessels that foundered.'

This return, your Petitioners would venture to remind your Honourable House, only applies to those wrecks or casualties occurring *on or near* the Coasts of the United Kingdom.

"That your Petitioners apprehend that the provisions proposed by clause 644 of the Bill, to render it a misdemeanour to send a ship to sea in an unseaworthy state, would be found practically inoperative. Your Petitioners believe that it would only require a small addition to the present number of the Marine Board of Trade Surveyors to perform the duty of inspection, and that it would be found better to prevent the sailing of an unseaworthy ship, rather than endeavour to punish the persons supposed to be responsible for a loss after its occurrence, and when proof of unworthiness would be next to, if not altogether, unobtainable.

"That your Petitioners regret that no provision is made in the Bill to determine the maximum load-line of ships and steamers. Recent experience has shown how much property is lost, and how many valuable lives are sacrificed, by overloading. The extent of the evil arising from such cause, in the absence of all inquiry into vessels lost at sea (except in some isolated cases), cannot be estimated, and your Petitioners feel that legislative measures alone can lessen this evil, and that the proposed provision of sec. 313, recording the draught of water of a sea-going ship, is insufficient, and that none of the proposals herein made can be held to relieve the ship-owner from his existing responsibility. Your Petitioners would observe, that however perfect the measure may otherwise be, if it be without distinct provisions to meet the evils resulting from overloading, it fails to deal with one of the most distinct and recognised deficiencies in the Merchant Shipping Service.

. " Competent authorities on Shipping agree upon the necessity for a line of extreme loading being defined.

" Your Petitioners venture to suggest that the Bill should provide, that for vessels hereafter to be built, such line might be determined by the Builder, in conjunction with the Surveyor of Lloyd's or the Surveyor to the Liverpool Underwriters' Association (under whichever inspection built), together with a Surveyor of the Board of Trade, a combination which would at once represent the Ship-owner, the Underwriter, and the Government, and that the decision of such body should be submitted to, and approved by the Board of Trade ; and that for vessels built under the inspection of neither of the above-mentioned Associations (a very rare exception), the Builder and Board of Trade Surveyor should determine such extreme limit of flotation, with power to call an Assessor under the Admiralty County Court Jurisdiction Act, in case of any disagreement.

" For vessels already navigating, the Builder and Surveyor of such ships, when practicable, together with a Surveyor of the Board of Trade, should fix such load-line, subject to the approval of the Board of Trade ; and, when this arrangement is impracticable, the Owner to appoint a representative, who, in conjunction with either the Surveyor of Lloyd's or to the Liverpool Underwriters' Association, and the Surveyor to the Board of Trade, should be called to determine such line.

"Your Petitioners would venture to call attention to the rules recently revised by Lloyd's, and published last month, upon the construction of Iron Ships, wherein it is said that —' As the safety and seaworthiness of Spar-decked vessels greatly depend upon the draught of water to which they are loaded, it is to be understood that the foregoing rules for their construction are framed with a view to their being loaded to such a draught *only* as will give a minimum free-board for every foot depth of hold, from the top of the floor-plate to the upper side of main or middle-deck beam of 1¼ inches, measured from the main or middle-deck stringer plate to the water's edge.'

"Your Petitioners would observe that the free-board, which this rule provides for, in the case of Spar-decked ships (a class of shipping, the construction of which is increasing, and, when not overloaded, the safest), closely corresponds with the opinions obtained by your Petitioners from the leading Ship Builders, Ship Surveyors, and Nautical Authorities of this District, and given in a report on the Merchant Shipping Bill, presented by this Chamber to the Board of Trade in November last.

"The limit determined upon might be stamped amidships, and the allowed free-board be recorded in a printed Certificate, posted on some [convenient part of the ship, in the same manner as is now done in Passenger ships, with regard to the number of passengers they are allowed to carry.

"That your Petitioners would point out that, while Practical Authorities hold that, in Spar-decked vessels, the line of immersion should be *below* the line of the main deck—the distance between the water's edge and the line of the main deck being regulated according to the depth of hold and build of vessel—yet, in practice, instances of loss of life and property, through being submerged *above* the

main deck, have come within your Petitioners' knowledge.

" That the increasing number of losses which takes place,
as your Petitioners believe, from preventible causes, has led
to an advance in the rates of premium of Insurance; thus
inflicting upon the Mercantile and Manufacturing Com-
munity a tax which, your Petitioners believe, care and
supervision might, to a certain extent, remedy and remove.

" That the principle which your Petitioners urge for
adoption is already admitted by Parliament in the Mines
and Factories Inspection, and other Acts. . . . ."

The Town Council of Leith had petitioned against the
practice of overloading on the foundering of the *Ivanhoe*
from this cause. About the same time also the Associated
Chambers of Commerce, through their representatives,
urged their views on this subject upon the attention of
the Government in the following terms :—

" 1. That a periodical inspection of all sailing ships and
steam ships, not carrying passengers, unclassed at Lloyd's,
or by the Liverpool Underwriters' Association, should be
compulsory.

" 2. That in consequence of the frequent losses of sailing and steam ships from the practice of *overloading*" [the
italics their own], "the associated chambers are of opinion
that the attention of the Government should be drawn to
this subject, and that it should be invited to take into consideration whether this Bill should not contain provisions
for determining the maximum load-line of sailing and steam
ships."

Now, what Chambers of Commerce are they who thus
express their wishes and opinions? Their names ought to
be printed in letters of gold. They are Dundee, Newcastle-
on-Tyne, West Hartlepool, Middlesboro', Stockton-on-Tees,
Goole, Hull, Southampton, Exeter, Plymouth, Falmouth,
Bristol, Gloucester, and Cardiff.

Thus, you see, nearly all the great ports not only sanction
but ask for this most salutary change in the law. In these

H

places the wonder is that nothing has been done before, but the explanation has already been given. Before insurance no law was necessary, and the changed condition of affairs has not yet sufficiently attracted the public attention.

At the meeting at which these resolutions were adopted, they were proposed by Mr. James Hall (of the firm of Palmer and Hall, the large ship-owners), of Newcastle-upon-Tyne, and he supported them in a speech so full of information, so pregnant with statements which would hardly be deemed authentic from any other than one himself a ship-owner and therefore fully conversant with the subject dealt with, and so honourable to his high feeling as a British merchant, that I give it in its entirety from the only copy I have, merely printing in italics the parts more especially deserving of notice.

[MERCHANT SHIPPING BILL.

Meeting of the Associated Chambers of Commerce, February, 1870, at the Westminster Palace Hotel, London.

> " That a periodical inspection of all sailing ships and steam ships, not carrying passengers, unclassed at Lloyd's, or by the Liverpool Underwriters' Association, should be compulsory."

Mr. JAMES HALL, of Newcastle, said—In asking the Associated Chambers of Commerce to adopt the resolution which has just been read, I regret that I have no data to put before you as to the extent of the evil which it is intended to remedy. *The knowledge that unseaworthy ships are allowed to navigate is best known to those who, like myself, are engaged in the maritime commerce of the country. I know of no case where an enquiry has been held into the loss of any ship which may have foundered at sea, with all hands, passenger ships excepted,* and in the absence of all such enquiries it is impossible to form any estimate. That the evil is a serious one I have no doubt. The class of shipping which is engaged in the coal trade, as a general rule, is a very inferior class. In the Mining Act the most stringent rules are laid down for the safety of those employed. If an accident happens, notice within twenty-four hours must be given to the Home Secretary, and where the consequences are attended with the loss of a single life, the inquest cannot be held until the inspector under the Government be present. How very different* is this state of things to

---

* Consider the difference.—S. P.

that of shipping; *one vessel after another may founder, with all hands, and not the least enquiry is made into the cause of their loss!* The proprietor of a colliery has, moreover, a direct interest in maintaining his property in the highest state of efficiency, for he has no Insurance Company to fall back upon to recoup him the damages which he may have sustained, whereas the same thing cannot always be said of the shipowner. It has been urged that the adoption of such a regulation by Government would relieve the responsibility of a shipowner. *I know of no case where a shipowner has been held responsible for sending his ship to sea in an unseaworthy condition.* It is further stated that it would entail the employment by Government of an army of surveyors. I am not of that opinion; an addition, it is true, but not a very considerable one, would suffice for the task. All the unclassed ships in the country, and it is with those only we propose to deal, are not to be found in port at one time. All passenger-carrying ships are at present periodically subject to an examination by a Board of Trade surveyor, and it is this same principle we propose should be extended to those vessels which are not classed at Lloyd's. I am not ignorant that many of our unclassed ships are classed with the French Veritas, but I feel that our Government would not be justified in recognising the classification of any foreign body. There are some shipowners who own first-class vessels who object to class their ships at Lloyd's, but their number is inconsiderable, and I feel quite sure that any such regulation as here proposed would by no means incommode them. *My own firm are managing owners of several large unclassed ships. I am not, therefore, wishing to impose upon others an inspection from which I myself would be exempt.* As a general rule, however, there is a reason, and sometimes a very cogent one, why owners object to have their vessels surveyed. For although a classification, however low the character might be that would be assigned by Lloyd's, would, in the most of cases, enhance the market value of such shipping, yet it is not to be doubted there are ships to which, in their present condition, not even the lowest class could be assigned. It is sometimes said that the question is an underwriter's question. It is so, to a limited extent only. *We have ships engaged in our coasting trade, and, to some extent, in our oversea trade, which are not insured at all, and some which would not be insured by any respectable company but at such a premium as would be totally prohibitory.* The calls made by some of the north-country clubs covering such risks have reached the enormous premium *of 25 to 30 per cent.*, and the clubs have almost all collapsed in consequence. The cause which has led to the collapsing of these clubs, is of itself sufficient to show the necessity there exists for interference on the part of Government, to step in and check an evil which involves the lives of our fellow men. I have referred to the absence of all data to estimate the extent of the evil, by reason of there seldom or never being any official enquiry into the loss of vessels of this character which have foundered at sea. I must, from my own personal experience, state, as director of one of our insurance offices, the case of a ship where the master and some of the crew left, and others were appointed, and when they started upon their voyage the vessel was so leaky that before she got out of the river she had to put back, and the cargo had to be discharged. The coals were sold, but the proceeds scarcely exceeded the expense incurred. A claim was made against our company for a total loss of the cargo, and, to prevent a costly lawsuit, we had to compromise the claim. If the vessel had proceeded to sea she might have foundered with all on board, and no official enquiry would ever have been instituted into her condition previous to sailing. I might refer to the case of a vessel lost on the east coast, which we were fortunately, from circumstances which afterwards came to our knowledge, able to show had been from the outset unseaworthy; *but, in defending the action brought against us by the owner, the law expenses exceeded three times the amount insured in our office.* If this vessel had foundered with all hands, we should have known nothing of the circumstances which afterwards came to our knowledge. I might also refer you to several other cases of vessels foundering, immediately after leaving port, from preventible causes. I might further refer you to the case of a ship that went ashore on the coast of Holland, that broke up so rapidly as to call forth the following remarks in a foreign journal:—" *The barque ———, laden with coals, was lost to the east of the harbour. The crew, consisting of seven men, were brought on shore. Two hours after the vessel struck there was nothing left of her but fragments. There were then seven lives which most probably would have been sacrificed had it taken more than two hours to have got them off. In order that a vessel should go to pieces in so short a time on a shore like ours, she must be in a most unseaworthy state, and we cannot understand how the English Government, so careful of the lives of its subjects, should allow certain shipowners, from mere motives of avarice, to send vessels to sea with almost a certainty of their being lost. We earnestly wish, for the sake of the brave English crews of the colliers, that their Government would do something for their security, by naming a special Commission to inspect their vessels.*" How frequently would those pertinent remarks apply to similar instances occurring upon our own shores, and where the lives are lost, instead of happily saved, as in this instance. Speaking as an underwriter, we are sometimes called upon to insure the cargo for a customer, who has no interest in the body of the ship, and although we have gone on increasing the premium until it is doubled, we have, from the frequent losses in some trades, lately resolved to decline such risks altogether. *Many of our coasting vessels, to my own knowledge, have to pump while in harbour, pump while at sea, and when overtaken by a heavy gale of wind, too frequently perish with all on board.* I have been for many years engaged in loading ships in the coasting trade, and *many are the faces of those captains, whose vessels I have loaded, who have gone to sea never to return again to port.* Strange as it may appear, men who are accustomed to trade between two ports will, *for the advantage of being frequently at their homes,* incur the risk of navigating such ships.* *In France, no vessel considered unseaworthy by the authorities is allowed to leave port.* The question is essentially a Government question; for I take it to be the first duty of Government to protect the lives of its subjects, and I observe that in introducing the Bill, Mr. Shaw Lefevre proposed an amendment, that it should be a misdemeanour to send a ship to sea in an unseaworthy state. Surely it would be far better to provide against such a loss by proper inspection before sailing, rather than to wait until the calamity

---

* Thus the best feelings of the poor men, the feelings which do them most honour, are made the lures to their own destruction.—S. P.

has occurred, and then to punish the shipowner. Moreover, the difficulty of proving a ship that was lost to have been unseaworthy, would practically make the clause of non-effect. I trust I have said sufficient to induce the Chamber to adopt the resolution under consideration.

(Carried unanimously.)

> "That, in consequence of the frequent losses of sailing and steam ships from the practice of *overloading*, the Associated Chambers are of opinion that the attention of the Government should be drawn to this subject, and that it should be invited to take into consideration whether the Bill should not contain provisions for determining the maximum load-line of sailing and steam ships."

Mr. JAMES HALL said—The resolution which has just been read is one the importance of which cannot be overestimated. However great may be the evil of sending unseaworthy ships to sea, *that of sending large and valuable steamers to sea overloaded, and consequently unseaworthy, involve consequences of the greatest magnitude. It is not too much to say that to this growing and increasing evil, hundreds—it may be thousands—of valuable lives,* and hundreds of thousands of pounds of valuable property *are annually sacrificed.* Again, I should like to have been able to put before you some data as to the extent of the evil, but in *the absence of all enquiry into steamers lost at sea, save in the case of passenger ships,* or some exceptional case, we are without data to form an estimate. *I do not, however, hesitate to say that, were an official appointed for a short time at some of our principal ports, to note the condition in which ships are sent on their voyage, a state of things would be revealed little creditable to us as a nation. I feel quite sure that the question is one which must sooner or later force itself upon the attention of the Government.* The resolution which I submit for the adoption of this body does not involve this meeting in defining or determining any arbitrary line for summer or winter. It may not be out of place if I call your attention to the report which lies upon your table, adopted by the Chamber which I represent, and in which will be found the opinions upon this subject of shipbuilders, some of whom are the largest and most practical in England, of practical ship surveyors, and experienced nautical men. You will there notice that no vessel can be deemed seaworthy that is sent to sea with less than two to three inches, counting from top of deck plank to water line, for every foot of depth of hold in the case of non-spar-decked ships; that is, for example, a ship with a depth of hold of eighteen feet, according to some authorities, should have a side or free board of three feet; according to some, three feet nine inches; and according to others, four and a half feet; and *in the case of spar-decked ships, no ship should be immersed above one to two feet, according to the views of the writers, below the main deck line. Yet it is not too much to say that these rules are daily violated. We have instances of vessels sent to sea almost flush midships with the water's edge,* and in the case of *spar-decked ships submerged above the main deck, instead of having a side or free board of from one to two feet or more below the main deck.* A friend of mine went, a few months ago, on board of a ship while she was loading, and asked the mate if he intended to sink her. The mate observed he did not intend to sail in her. *The ship proceeded next morning, and the only vestige heard of her since has been a small part of her outfit cast up in the channel, indicating the sad end of ship and crew.* I may refer to the case of another steamer, whose condition, as she proceeded to sea, was such as to be the theme of conversation amongst all nautical men. She foundered, with the loss of all hands, almost, it is supposed, immediately after leaving harbour. A few days ago I found .that a steamer I had chartered had loaded more than was expected. The captain was asked the reason, when he replied that the *loading had been attended to by his owner, but he himself wished so much cargo had not been put on board.* One who saw the vessel subsequently reported to me that she had very little side or free board. *On the Friday the vessel left the Tyne, and on the Sunday night following a loss off the Norfolk coast was reported, and a boat washed up bearing the name of this very ship.* There is only too much reason to fear that she had been lost, with all hands. I might refer to the cases of spar-decked ships so deeply laden as to have their main deck under water, and foundering after leaving port. In the case of passenger ships the Government determine the number of passengers they may carry, but do not determine, what is of much more importance, the draught of water the same vessel should draw; and passenger-carrying ships may, in this the month of February, be seen leaving our ports with the arch board on the stern of the ships upon which the ship's name and port are generally painted, on a line with the water's edge. *The wonder is, not that so many ships are lost, but that the number is so few.* In the case of the *Ivanhoe*, it was alleged that some of the crew would not proceed, and others were shipped, and within *twenty-four hours after sailing, it is supposed, she foundered, with all hands.* The Town Council of Leith, if I mistake not, on that occasion passed such a resolution as the one I now submit for your adoption. We are told that it is impossible to fix such line, and that it cannot be done. Practical men who have thought over the matter think otherwise. Lloyd's, as you are aware, are supposed to have a standing rule that every ship should have a side or free board of 3 inches to the foot of depth of hold. This, however, does not apply to spar-decked ships. And the rule of 3 inches to the foot is made compulsory by Government when Government stores are shipped by merchant vessels; and it might, therefore, almost be imagined that *stores were deemed by Government more valuable than the lives of subjects.* The Newcastle Chamber suggested that, in the event of the Legislature not seeing fit to fix a basis, a line should be determined by the builder of the ship, the inspector, under whichever book she was built, and the Board of Trade surveyor; their decision to be subject to the Board of Trade. It would, I think, be impossible to devise a more able and unbiassed tribunal to determine such line. In my opinion, a line marking the extreme limit of flotation compatible with safety should be fixed. It may be argued that such line would relieve the owner's responsibility, *but my experience is,* whether responsible or not, *to my knowledge no shipowner has ever been called upon to account for any misdoing in this respect. It has been said that such a rule would shackle us in competing with the foreign shipowner.* IF OUR SUCCESS HAS TO BE PURCHASED BY SACRIFICING THE LIVES OF OUR SAILORS, THE FOREIGNER, FOR MY

---

* She was lost with all hands.—S. P.

[PART,. IS WELCOME TO THE TRADE ;* but in this case the foreigner
is a myth. He does not exist. The steam-carrying trade of this country
and Europe is at present, and likely to remain, in the hands of British
shipowners. Competition exists among ourselves, and a very sharp one
it is becoming. It is said it is an underwriter's question. An underwriter meets increased risks by increased premiums, and the owner who
does not overload his vessel in the end has to pay for him who does.
It has also been said that the question might be safely left to those who
navigate them. There will never be wanting volunteers to man a
vessel, however deeply she may be laden—the *Ivanhoe* to wit. *I
speak as a steam shipowner, and say that the carrying out of the resolution under consideration would be deemed by many amongst us as no
unjust interference, and as imposing no harsh restriction upon our
property !!* Many of us feel *that such a rule has become a necessity;*
while to those who practise the evil, which it would to a certain extent
remedy, it would be an effectual barrier. *There is a reluctance
amongst most men to speak out upon this subject.*† But the Government themselves have admitted the necessity by suggesting, as an
amendment measure, for taking the draught of water on sailing, but
the same argument before used will apply; *it is prevention, preventing
overloading before sailing, which is required, and not future punishment,* or furnishing means for underwriters to resist claims for loss.
The draught of water a vessel draws can now at any time be procured
at the office of the pilots. I hope you will adopt the resolution.
*Sooner or later it must be adopted by the Government, and, in the in-
terest of humanity, the sooner that period arrives the better.*]

But what says Liverpool? Now, many would think, and
think reasonably, that great weight ought to be attached to
the opinion of Liverpool, as it is by far the largest port in
the world. Well, I am more glad than I can say to be able
to show you what Liverpool thinks not only on the subject
generally, but on the provisions of the Bill introduced by
me last year.

This is a cutting from the *Shipping and Mercantile
Gazette,* under date June 7, 1870, and is the letter of a

* Hear, hear! Bravo, James Hall!—S. P.
† There is little to be surprised at in this, as it is within my knowledge that a most worthy and large-hearted man who did venture to
speak freely of some instances of wrong-doing, was prosecuted for
libel in the Criminal Court, and actually sent to gaol for some months;
and at whose suit, do you think? Why, there may be two persons of
the same name, of course, but the name of the prosecutor was the
name of one of the men whose ships insurance brokers had to engage
not to put goods into when they offered to insure produce or goods for
shipment, the ships for which had not yet been chartered; thus,
" Warranted not to be loaded into ships belonging to ——— ———."
—S. P.

gentleman well known in Liverpool, and thoroughly well acquainted with shipping business.

[LOAD-DRAUGHT OF MERCHANT SHIPS.

To the Editor of the SHIPPING AND MERCANTILE GAZETTE.

SIR,—In my letters to you on this subject, I have stated that iron vessels of ordinary proportions show 30 per cent. "spare buoyancy" when their free-board is one-fourth of their depth of hold, and that, when the form of a vessel differs from these proportions, the divergence (so far as load-draught is concerned) is indicated by the difference which exists between the builder's tonnage and the registered tonnage. Further, I have suggested that this difference may be taken as a guide to the proportion by which the free-board of a shallow and fine, or of a deep, or of a full and deep, vessel should vary from the usual scales for load-draught ; and, by way of illustration, I have compared the free-board of several spar-decked vessels as modified in accordance with this suggestion. I also called the attention of your readers to the fact, that the difference between 25 per cent. and 30 per cent. of "spare buoyancy" is much more important than it at first sight appears ; as, for iron vessels of ordinary proportions as to breadth and depth, it means a scale for free-board of $2\frac{1}{2}$ inches, instead of three inches, for each foot depth of hold.

Mr. Plimsoll, in his Bill " to provide for greater security of life at sea," fairly "takes the bull by the horns," so far as load-draught is concerned, by proposing a fixed load-line—that is, an arbitrary load-line—beyond which a vessel may not load. It is not pretended that a vessel may not load more deeply, and yet make a safe voyage under ordinary circumstances ; * but the Bill avoids the discussion of these circumstances : it says, so far may a given vessel be loaded, but no further, except under penalty ; and in this respect all British Shipowners shall be placed on the same footing. *Mr. Plimsoll's proposal has met with a large amount of support from the Owners of sailing vessels in this town. The Committee of the Liverpool Shipowners' Association have, I understand, unanimously supported this part of the Bill, as they consider that, while the restrictions upon loading will not affect those who already load their ships reasonably, it will act as a decided check on the unscrupulous Owner or Charterer,* and will tend, by the greater safety which will follow, to reduce the general rate of Marine Insurance. As high-class Shipowners are thus in favour of a fixed load-line, the Bill may possibly *receive more support than was at first expected.* It seems, however, unnecessary that the proposed mark amidships should be so long as four feet, or that any load-mark should be painted at the bow and stern. A mark amidships on each side of a vessel, of one foot in length, would be ample for the purpose intended, as, whatever the difference may be in a vessel's trim, the load-draught is always referred to in the midship immersion by taking a mean of the draught indicated at the bow and stern. The trim of a vessel may safely be left discretionary, as there can be no inducement adverse to the interests of the public, or to those of the crew of a vessel, to put her

---

* Fair weather, I presume.—S. P.

out of trim. The mark amidships will limit the weight the vessel is to carry, and there are usually other considerations, such as Pilotage Dues, which are paid on the maximum draught, and the depth of water on bars, dock sills, &c., which induce owners to keep their vessels as nearly as may be on an even keel. As the other parts of Mr. Plimsoll's Bill do not relate to the subject of my present correspondence, I refrain here from making any comment upon them.

Yours obediently,

Liverpool, June 4, 1870.   W. W. RUNDELL.]

As to the other ports of the kingdom I can't speak, but am of opinion they would all welcome legislative interference with the practices complained of, as (and that I cannot too often repeat) these evil practices are only the practices of a small minority of bad men.

You may say, " How is it, then, if there is no objection on the part of the ship-owners, that you have failed to carry your bill through Parliament?" "What influence is it which stands in the way?"

In reply I add that in North and South, in East and in West, wherever my inquiries have taken me—I really cannot call to mind, nor do I believe that a case has arisen—where any one person has failed to render me, when asked, most ready assistance, or has failed to express the most decided opinions on the necessity of legislative interference, together with the most earnest wishes for my success; and I have gone to any one likely to be able to give me the information I needed—ship-owners and ship-builders, underwriters and insurance brokers, dock-masters ahd captains of ships, Custom House authorities and river police, not one single person has refused ready assistance and best wishes.

But you must remember that these all have their own daily affairs to attend to, they cannot neglect these to give that earnest attention and time necessary to work a reform. And though they are many, and those who profit by these practices are few, there is this difference on the part of the latter—it is their business, that of the latter, to resist change; they profit by things as they are; they are determined, energetic, and sleeplessly vigilant.

You must remember large fortunes are being made by them; they are the most energetic and pushing men in the trade, and it should not be matter of surprise if three of them had even got into Parliament.

Now, I don't want to say a single word disrespectful to Parliament : it has been a matter of constant surprise to me, since I became acquainted with the amount of work a member has to do, that so many men of ample means should be willing to devote their whole time in the best part of the year to gratuitous labour, all of them too (but two or three) men of high character and humane feeling ; but, nevertheless, owing to the fact that two or three of what they call in the North "the greatest sinners in the trade," having got into the House, it is there, and there only, that opposition to reform is to be expected, or is found.

Without mentioning names perfectly well known in the sea-ports, I will give you an idea of what I mean.

In the year 1870, when my bill was before the House the first time, the evening appointed for the second reading arrived. I was standing in the lobby, when a member accosted me thus :—" Do you expect your bill will come on to-night?"

" Yes, I hope so," I said.

He said, " I am sorry for that, as I have a dinner engagement; but I should not like to be absent."

" I think you should not be absent," was my reply.

" Why?" said he sharply.

" Because," I said, " I may have to tell the House of a man, whose name you will hear in any coffee-room or exchange in Yarmouth, Hull, Scarborough, Whitby, Pickering, Blythe, Shields, Newcastle, Sunderland, or in any port on the north-east coast, as one notorious for excessive and habitual overloading, and a reckless disregard for human life, who has lost seven ocean-going steamers, and drowned more than a hundred men, in less than two years,* and

---

* No inquiry of course was held in any one of these cases.

whose name I have myself seen as one of those whose ships insurance brokers at Lloyd's at length warrant the under-writers they will not ship goods in, before the underwriters will take a line upon them, and I may have to tell the House that that man is the member for ———"

I thought the man would have fainted. He answered never a word.

Now he had put on the paper a notice to move an amend-ment to the second reading of my bill, viz., that it be read a second time that day six months. Every member knows that if such a purpose is abandoned, it is only necessary for the member who has given notice of the amendment to absent himself, or to sit still when his turn comes to speak —that is all.

Some twenty minutes after this interview (and another I shall speak of soon), I was in my place in a state of strong excitement, because I had just made two powerful enemies. I felt utterly alone in my work, and so sick with excitement and fear, that I was compelling myself to think of the poor widows I had seen to keep up my courage, when a hand was put upon my shoulder. Much startled, I looked round, and there stood this man, with a face like that of a dead man, and this is what he said :—

" Mr. Plimsoll, I have been to Mr. Palgrave and taken my notice off the paper."

Why did he go to Mr. Palgrave? Why did he trouble to tell me he had done so ?

The bill came on too late that night for consideration, and was put forward ; and when, early next day, I looked at the fresh issue of the order book, and looked amongst notices relating to orders of the day, that notice of amend-ment was not there !

I may say here that the bill, though frequently put down afterwards, never did come on that session, owing to the dreadful waste of the time of the House by incessant speech-making of members who cannot really speak but don't know it.

Those who can't, and do know it, seldom address the House but when they feel it is their plain duty.

After turning away from the member I have referred to, I encountered another, and told him that I thought he would do well to stay, because it was probable that I should refer to a case of a spar-decked ship being sent to Cronstadt in November with a cargo of iron, nearly twice as many tons as her register tonnage, with her main-deck between two and three feet under the water-line. He threatened me with an action for lible if I did; but the voters of Derby had made me strong enough to defy him. He said I had no right to name a matter relating to a member without giving him notice. I reminded him that I was then giving him notice. He said he would not take it; and finally, with a dark and deadly look, said, if I dared to allude to the case I must take the consequences. I was obliged to tell him that my duty was plain, and as to the consequences, I thought he was likely to take his share of them with me.

You will see, therefore, that I had sufficient reason for the agitation I was in when the first member made the astonishing and unnecessary (!) announcement that he had been to Mr. Palgrave and had taken his notice off the paper.

In 1871, when I brought in my bill a second time, it was most anxiously debated by me with myself whether or no I should allude to these cases. Hoping to succeed without doing so, I did not allude to them in my opening speech, and of course was then precluded from doing so in my reply, and these two men actually took advantage of this omission to speak against the bill, and put up another member, who would, I am afraid, find it very embarrassing to answer some questions that might be put to him.

These men, being all ship-owners, have of course great weight with the House, and I was obliged to withdraw my bill, taking as compensation only the bill subsequently brought in by the Board of Trade, which is worth nothing. It gives the seamen a right to ask for a survey, but they must pay all the expense of it if the surveyors certify that the ship is not unseaworthy.

Now, I do not want the inquiry I hope to obtain to become a trail-hunt after individuals ; our object must be to amend a bad system, and to keep well in mind that but for our own neglect so sad a state of things could not have arisen. I have merely adverted to these cases to indicate the quarter whence all the opposition we fear is to be expected. I have been in great perplexity too as to whether or no I should name these cases or not, and have decided to do so only from the fear that if I did not, these persons would probably still speak deprecating any change, and, being ship-owners, the House would be in danger of supposing they spoke the opinions of ship-owners, whereas this is not only not true, but the reverse is the fact, for the great body of ship-owners earnestly desire the legislation I advocate.

I think I have shown abundantly that there is not a powerful opposition to be feared. It will be seen that the recommendation of the Newcastle Chamber of Commerce is that *unclassed* ships shall be subject to compulsory survey—*mine* is that all should, with a schedule of exceptions ; the results would be precisely alike, except in this single particular—to make all subject, and then make exceptions when they can safely be made, is to affirm the principle of Government responsibility in the matter, which I think you will agree with me it is high time should be done.

But I was to explain what is meant by the term *unclassed.* Nearly all ships when new are fit to take valuable merchandise, as silks, tea, provisions, cloth, cutlery, stationery, &c. (goods which sea-water if it reached them would greatly injure), on long voyages, because she is "tight," *i.e.* not leaky, so she is classed A 1 by Lloyd's Committee. The letter refers to the ship, the numeral to the ship's equipment, as rigging, boats, cables, anchors, &c. ; but they are also classed for terms which vary with the quality of the timber used in building them, and the quality of the work-

manship is also taken into account.   Thus, speaking generally (because other timber may have been used in some
parts of the ship), if a ship be built mainly of hemlock,
yellow pine, beech, or fir, she will probably be classed A 1
for a term of four or five years; if of elm or ash, five to
six years; red pine or Cowdie Huon pine, six to seven
years; pitch pine or American white oak, seven to eight
years; oak (foreign), eight to nine years; and if of English
oak or teak (East Indian), nine to twelve years; subject
to what is called a half-time survey of a very strict and
thorough character, *i.e.* if classed for eight years, at the
end of four, and if classed for twelve years then at the
end of six years.   She may again at the request of the
owner be examined for continuation, *i.e.* to be continued in
this class for a further term, usually two-thirds of that originally granted.   She may again and again be re-examined
for continuation, or if she have meantime gone into a lower
class, be examined for restoration to the character A; but
each of these surveys is increased in thoroughness and
stringency as the age of the ship increases.   When from age
she ceases to be entitled to the character A in the opinion
of Lloyd's surveyor, but is still tight enough and strong
enough to carry valuable merchandise to any part of the
world, she is classed A red, usually for an original term of
half or two-thirds the original term granted her in the
first character.   She is still subject to half-time survey, and
may be surveyed and re-surveyed for continuation in this
class.   When from increasing age she is no longer fit to carry
valuable goods for long voyages, she falls into class black
diphthong Æ; while in this class she is deemed fit to carry
the same class of goods, but only on short voyages (not
beyond Europe).   And when after survey and re-survey at
intervals, as before, she is no longer fit to carry valuable
goods at all, she falls into class E, and is deemed fit only to
carry goods which sea-water won't hurt, as metallic ores,
coal, coke, &c. (and then she usually travels round from
Liverpool to an eastern port), for long voyages, that is,
anywhere, or is employed in the timber trade.   After survey

and re-surveys at intervals as before, she is deemed unfit to
go long voyages at all, and is only fit to carry materials not
capable of injury by sea-water on short voyages—she is then
classed 1; and when she has run through her terms here
she is said to have run out her classes, to be in fact an "unclassed ship." The lettering is slightly varied for iron ships:
thus, $\underset{\overline{A}}{A}$, $\underset{\overline{B}}{A}$, $\underset{\overline{C}}{A}$.

All this submitting to survey is entirely optional, and the
owner or builder may build as he likes, or repair or leave
unrepaired as he likes; and when this is so, these ships are
also called "unclassed ships."

Now, surely the merchants and ship-owners of Newcastle are not without reason when they affirm that all unclassed ships should be subjected to compulsory survey
before they are allowed to go to sea with a freight of precious
human life.

All the ships which are surveyed by Lloyd's are so surveyed to enable their owners to insure, and also to sell them
if needed, on better terms than they otherwise could.

How, then, do the owners of ships which have run through
all their classes, or which have been built anyhow, insure at
all? In this way. They mutually insure; they form
clubs, and a member paying an uncertain rate is indemnified by the others, upon all of whom at the end of the
year a call is made, depending upon the amount of the
year's losses; and well does Mr. Hall say that the state
of these clubs ought alone to have called attention long
ago to the nature of the ships insured, for they collapse
one after another after struggling along a few years; and,
indeed, it almost seems as if there were a race who should
lose his ships first on the formation of a new club, so
great are the sums the members are called upon to pay
as premium. In one afternoon alone in Newcastle once
I picked up the names of nearly a dozen which had collapsed within a few years after paying tremendous calls.
I call to mind the following now:—The Albion Mutual
Insurance Club, which failed in 1864; the Britannia, in
1865; the Shields Marine, in 1866; the Eligible, 1867; the

British, 1868; the Friendly, 1868; and the Ocean, which failed in 1870.

Some of these clubs failed after calling upon their members to pay 18 per cent., 20 per cent., and 25 per cent.; and one of them failed after calling upon its members to pay 18 per cent. in one year on the amounts for which they had entered their vessels, and in the next year no less than 30 per cent., showing conclusively how utterly unseaworthy these vessels were—they had only three years of life in them on the average, and yet we allow such vessels to go to sea, taking fathers of families and others with them ! I am told also that 40 per cent. has repeatedly been called by these mutual assurance clubs.

I have now explained, I hope, what "unclassed" means, and given you some idea of the nature of unclassed ships, and now my task is nearly done.

I have shown you that what Mr. O'Dowd, the counsel of the Board of Trade, justly calls a "homicidal system," exists in our midst ; that it is vain to look to underwriters for a remedy ; that it is equally vain to expect it from the poor sailors themselves ; that the ship-owners as a class have done all they can ; and that, therefore, it is your duty, yours personally, and mine, to endeavour to apply a remedy.

I have also shown you that in extending to our fellow-men at sea the protection of the law we should not be setting a precedent, but should simply be following many precedents long established, only giving the sailors what we ashore have long enjoyed.

I have shown you the extent of the evil, examined its sources, distinguishing those requiring skilled treatment from those you can pronounce upon.

I have indicated to you the almost total change which will follow if we do our duty.

I have shown you how utterly groundless are all the objections urged against doing our simple duty ; and, finally, that nearly all the ports are earnestly desirous of our assistance.

And now I'll tell you what I propose to do in the coming Session, and earnestly beg your assistance :—

I shall bring in a Bill providing for the compulsory survey of all merchant ships (the Newcastle proposal and mine are alike in effect, as you have seen), and providing also that no ship shall be allowed to proceed to sea overloaded, giving the ship-owner the choice of all existing scales, subject to approval by the Board of Trade.

Whether there will be a third clause, dealing with over-insurance, will depend upon the advice of practical men in the meantime. The sum for which a ship may fairly be assured must be a fixed sum per ton register, and the amount will necessarily vary with the ship's class, her age, rig, and material. It will be a work of time and difficulty to arrange schedules dealing with this point. I shall seek the best practical aid available, and if the thing can be accomplished on going into it, in time—well ; if not, my Bill will only deal with overloading and rottenness, except this point, the master must be made to return the number of hands he has on board on proceeding to sea,—with a view to future legislation, if it is found necessary.

I shall also move an address to the Crown, praying Her Majesty to issue a Royal Commission to inquire into the other sources of loss I have referred to, and into the general subject; but we must not allow even the issue of such a commission to delay legislation if we can help it on these two points, on which we are as able to pronounce as any commission, namely,—*That* ships unseaworthy by reason of want of repair shall not be allowed to go to sea unrepaired ; and that ships shall not be overloaded.

With reference to the first point, I have this day heard (Dec. 13, 1872) of a very bad case. The owners of a ship (I am not at liberty to mention her name or her owners) applied to Lloyd's to have her classed. She was surveyed, and reported to be in a bad condition, two or three material defects being obvious. Lloyd's Committee refused to give her any class in her then condition ; the owners pressed—

I

the matter was gone into again. The Committee referred again to the surveyor. He said in reply, "She is utterly unfit to go to sea, unless the defects (specified) are attended to." The owners refused to lay out any money; she was refused classification. She was loaded in London, and went on her voyage to cross the Atlantic. Going down the Thames the crew became aware of her state, and at Deal refused to proceed on the voyage. They were landed and taken to prison, and subsequently sentenced, one and all, to a long term of imprisonment in the county gaol. Another crew was obtained somehow, and the ship went on her voyage, and while the one set of men were in gaol, ail the others went to the bottom of the sea, for she was never heard of again. I can give all particulars to a Royal Commission, as well as of several other cases, all of them just as bad.

Now you who read these pages—somebody *shall* read them, if I have to give away the whole edition—will you help me to put these things right? If you will, whether man or woman, write me just a line to 111, Victoria Street, S.W., to say so, and I will then say how you best can do so. There is little reason, I fear, for thinking my correspondence will be too heavy for me, for no one seems to care for the sailors; but write, and I shall be able, I dare say, to say what is best to be done in your case.

If our sailors were as bad as bad can be, if their labour was of no use to any of us, that would surely be no reason for permitting such a "homicidal system" (Mr. O'Dowd) to continue; but they are not bad, they are as brave and manly fellows as any class ashore, and they have wives and families to deplore and suffer for their loss.

I would with all my heart and soul that I possessed the eloquence of Bright, the graphic power of MM. Erckmann-Chatrian, to use in their behalf, for then you would surely be moved to action; but I have not, yet I may tell you why I feel so strongly on their behalf. If the lives of nearly a thousand of our ministers of religion, or of our lawyers, or of our doctors, or of our public men were sacrificed every year, to what a Government officer described as a "homicidal system," to pure and most culpable neglect, what would be said? All England would ring with indignation at the outrage; yet I venture to say, and I say it conscientiously, believing it to be true, that any thousand of what is called the working classes are as worthy of respect and affection as any of these. If honesty, if strong aversion to idleness, if tenderness to wife and children, if generosity to one another in adversity, and if splendid courage are claims to respect, I am not sure that, taking them as a whole, you can find these moral qualities in equal degree in any other class.

I don't wish to disparage the rich, but I think it may be reasonably doubted whether these qualities are so fully developed in them; for, notwithstanding that not a few of them are not unacquainted with the claims, reasonable and unreasonable, of poor relations, these qualities are not in such constant exercise, and riches seem in so many cases to smother the manliness of their possessors, and their sympathies become not so much narrowed as, so to speak, stratified—they are reserved for the sufferings of their own class, and also the woes of those above them. They seldom tend downwards much, and they are far more likely to admire an act of high courage, like that of the engine-driver who saved his passengers lately from an awful collision by cool courage, than to admire the constantly exercised fortitude and the tenderness which are the daily characteristics of a British workman's life.

You may doubt this. I once should have done so myself, but I have shared their lot; I have lived with them. For months and months I lived in one of the model lodging-houses, established mainly by the efforts of Lord Shaftesbury—there is one in Fetter Lane, another in Hatton Garden, and indeed they are scattered all over London. I went there simply because I could not afford a better lodging. I have had to make 7s. 9½d. (3s. of which I paid for my lodging) last me a whole week, and did it. It is astonishing how little you can live on, when you divest yourself of all fancied needs. I had plenty of good wheat bread to eat all the week, and the half of a herring for a relish (less will do if you can't afford half, for it is a splendid fish), and good coffee to drink; and I know how much, or rather how little, roast shoulder of mutton you can get for 2*d.* for your Sunday's dinner. Don't suppose I went there from choice—I went of stern necessity (and this was promotion too), and I went with strong shrinking, with a sense of suffering great humiliation, regarding my being there as a thing to be carefully kept secret from all my old friends. In a word, I considered it only less degrading than spunging upon friends, or borrowing what I saw no chance of ever being able to pay.

Now what did I see there? I found the workmen considerate for each other. I found that they would go out (those who were out of employment) day after day, and patiently trudge miles and miles seeking employment, returning night after night unsuccessful and dispirited; only, however, to sally out the following morning with renewed determination. They would walk incredibly long distances, to places where they heard of a job of work; and this not for a few days, but for many, many days. And I have seen such a man sit down wearily by the fire (we had a common room for sitting and cooking everything), with a hungry, despondent look—he had not tasted food all day—and accosted by another, scarcely less poor than himself, with " Here, mate, get this into thee," handing him at the same time a piece of bread and some cold meat, and afterwards some coffee. And adding, " Better luck tomorrow; keep up your pecker." And all this without any idea that they were practising the most splendid patience, fortitude, courage, and generosity I had ever seen. You would hear them talk of absent wife and children sometimes—these in a distant workhouse (trade was very bad then) with expressions of affection, and the hope of seeing them again soon; although the one was irreverently alluded to as " my old woman," and the latter as " the kids."

I very soon got rid of miserable self-pity there, and came to reflect that Dr. Livingstone would probably be thankful

for good wheat bread ; and, if the bed was of flock and
hay, and the sheets of cotton, that better men than I in the
Crimea (the war was going on then) would think themselves
very lucky to have as good ; and then, too, I began to
reflect, that when you come to think of it, that such as these
men were, so were the vast majority of the working classes;
that the idle and the drunken we see about publichouses
are but a small minority of them, made to appear more
because publichouses are all put in such places ; that the
great bulk are at home—for the man who has to be at work
at six in the morning can't stay up at night ; he is in bed
early, and is as I found my fellow-inmates. Now just consider : do you not—unconsciously, it may well be—still, do
you not sometimes, in thinking of working men, picture
those, few though they be, you see late at night about
publichouses ; not exclusively, perhaps, but rather more
than of the ninety and nine who are at home with their
families, recruiting their physical strength for the morrow's
work ? Well, it was impossible to indulge self-pity in circumstances like these, and, emulous of the genuine manhood
all around me, I set to work again ; for what might not be
done with youth and health ? and simply by preparing
myself rather more thoroughly for my business than had
previously been considered necessary, I was soon strong
enough to live more in accordance with my previous life,
and am now able to speak a true word for the genuine men
I left behind, simply because my dear parents had given me
greater advantages than these men had had. But I did not
leave all at once. I wanted to learn the lesson well ; and,
though I went reluctantly, I remained voluntarily, because
the kindly feelings I took with me had changed into hearty
respect and admiration, and I was busy thinking, for some
things I thought I knew before appeared in a new and
different aspect—for instance, I knew that when the explosion took place at the Warren Vale Colliery, that as a
member of the relief committee, formed in Sheffield, I had
found that the claims upon the funds had not been limited
to the wives and children of the poor men killed, but we

found that in several instances the men killed had supported
widowed mothers, and in others younger brothers and
sisters, who had with themselves been deprived of fathers
by some preceding accident.   And, again, at the Lund Hill
explosion this was the case too—nearly one-third of the
men killed, as the respective committees can testify, were
thus supporting relations others than wife or child.

Have you reflected what this is ?   Rich men, even com-
fortably-to-do men, do this, I don't doubt.   But consider
the difference ; in one case it is simply signing a cheque,
and mayhap leaving rather less behind him ; in the other,
it is perhaps having rather less to spend on what, after all,
perhaps is foregone without any personal discomfort ; but
in the case of the collier every shilling thus spared means
more than an hour's hard work, lying nearly naked on his
side in a solitary benk or heading far away from the pit-
bottom, with his life literally in the keeping of each one of
all the many men working in the pit.

I also thought a little more of the subscriptions of the
men I had generally managed at the brewery where I was
employed before I came to London to seek my fortune.
And the more I thought the more I wondered at the readi-
ness with which men earning 16*s.* per week, and a cottage,
and having a wife, and, in some cases, five, and seven children, would spare 1*s.* each to help a dead comrade's widow,
or 6*d.* to help a fellow-workman to defray the extra expense
of a funeral in his family.   Fancy what a sum 1*s.* is in such
circumstances !

I thought, too, of the wonderful courage—more : of the
real and wonderful heroism of the working men in circumstances of peril—deadly peril—at Edmund's Main Colliery
explosion, when nearly two hundred men perished.   After
the first explosion, and a second was expected every moment, there was some doubt whether all in the pit were
killed.   "Who volunteers to go down to search ?" is asked.
Instantly, and without any knowledge apparently that the act
was out of the common way, three times the number of men
wanted stepped forward and went down.   They never came

up again alive, poor fellows, for a second explosion came, and the brave and gallant men, though their faces and hands were black, vindicated their courage with their lives.

Again, when the last explosion took place at the Oaks Colliery, and it was thought some might be living below, when my dear friend, Parkin Jeffcock, held up his hand, and said, " Well, lads, who goes down WITH me ? "—(that's the place of an English gentleman,) more than double the number he wanted quickly stepped out of the crowd. God help me, I fear I should not have the like courage in like circumstances, for a second explosion was so imminent that, having selected his men, the rest were ordered to fall back from the pit's mouth, lest they should be blown into the air. You know they never came up again. Poor fellows ! Poor Jeffcock ! it was a death worthy of envy almost as much as Cobden's life was.

Who forgets Joe Rodgers, the plain seaman, who, with a thin cord made fast to his body, sprang from the deck of the *Royal Charter*, on the chance that he might be dashed on the shore with life enough to establish the line which was stretched from ship to shore, and which saved nearly forty lives ? or the sailor who, when the Sailors' Home, which the late Prince Albert assisted to build in Liverpool, was ablaze, and the ladders were all too short to reach the highest floor, where the sailors were shut up by the fire, took one ladder, with the bottom rung resting on the bend of his right arm, and, pushing it up before him, mounted to the top of another, and thus, at the extreme peril of his own life (for had the imprisoned sailors not come down one at once all would have been killed), saved the lives of five men ?

Can we forget the common soldiers too, who, when the *Birkenhead* was lost, went down to death, shoulder to shoulder, having to the last kept their ranks to form a pathway of safety to the women and children ?

Remember the *Sarah Sands*, too. Death seems robbed of all its horror when it is accompanied by glories like these. And now, tell me if I have not reason when I say that I absolutely glory in the working men, and aspire no higher

than to merit equal respect with them.   Yes, before I left
my friends—for such we became at the model lodging-house
—I had learned to feel as well as to know that—

> " Honour and shame from no condition rise :
>   Act well your part, there all the honour lies ; "

and had also become more fully aware than I was before,
how great and how glorious a thing it is to be born an Eng-
lishman.   And yet these are the men we leave, shamefully
leave, to perish by the dozen, by the score, without an effort
to save them—allow them to perish from causes which could
be remedied before the winter of 1873, and yet make no effort.

Do you want to know more about the sort of men who
thus are cut off in their full manhood ?   Do you want to
know how their loss is felt ?   Come with me a few minutes,
and I'll show you.   The initials are all strictly correct, both
those indicating names and also those giving addresses, and
I can produce all the people.   In this house, No. 9, L——ll
Street, lives Mrs. A——r R——e.   Look at her; she is not
more than two- or three-and-twenty, and those two little ones
are hers.   She has a mangle, you see.   It was subscribed
for by her poor neighbours—the poor are very kind to each
other.   That poor little fellow has hurt his foot, and looks
wonderingly at the tearful face of his young mother.   She
had a loving husband but very lately ; but the owner of the
ship, the *S——n*, on which he served, was a very needy
man, who had insured her for nearly £3,000 more than she
had cost him ; so, if she sank, he would gain all this.   Well,
one voyage she was loaded *under the owner's personal super-
intendence;* she was loaded so deeply that the dock-master
pointed her out to a friend as she left the dock, and said
emphatically, " That ship will never reach her destination."
She never did, but was lost with all hands, twenty men and
boys.   A—— R—— complained to her before he sailed,
that the ship was " so deep loaded."   She tried to get to the
sands to see the ship off with Mrs. S——r, whose husband
also was on board.   They never saw their husbands again.

In this most evil-smelling room E—— Q——, C——

Street, you may see in the corner two poor women in one bed, stricken with fever (one died two days after I saw them), mother and daughter. The husband of the daughter, who maintained them both, had been lost at sea a little while before—a ship so loaded that when Mr. B——l, a Custom House officer, who had to go on board for some reason as she was lying in the river, on asking whereabouts the ship was, was told, "She's yonder; you can easily find her; she's nearly over t' head in water." Mr. B——l told me, "I asked no questions, but stepped on board. This description was quite sufficient."

Mrs. R——s, 14, H——n Place, told me her young brother was an orphan with herself. She and her sister had brought him up until she was married. Then her husband was kind to him, and apprenticed him to the sea. He had passed as second mate in a sailing ship; but (he was a fine young fellow : I have his portrait) he was ambitious to "pass in steam" also ; engaged to serve in the *S*—— ship, leaking badly, but was assured on signing that she was to be repaired before loading. The ship was not repaired, and was loaded, as he told his sister-mother, "like a sand-barge." Was urged by his sister, and also her husband, not to go. His sister again urged him, as he passed her bedroom door in the morning, not to go. He promised he wouldn't, and went to the ship to get the wages due to him. Was refused payment unless he went ; was over-persuaded, and threatened, and called a coward, which greatly excited him. He went; and two days afterwards the ship went down. Her husband, Mr. R——s, also told me that he and his wife "had a bit crack," and decided to do all they could "to persuade Johnnie not to go." The young man was about twenty-two.

Mr. J—— H——l told me that the captain was his friend, and the captain was very "down-hearted about the way she was loaded" (mind, she was loaded under the owner's personal supervision). The captain asked him (Mr. A——) to see his wife off by train after the ship had sailed. She, poor soul! had travelled to that port to see

him off. Captain said to him, " I doubt I'll never see her
more!" and burst out crying. Poor fellow! he never did
see her more.

Now come with me to 36, C—— Street, and see Mrs.
J——s R——e. She is a young woman of superior intelligence, and has a trustable face—very. She may be about
twenty-seven. She lost her husband in the same ship. He
was thirty years of age, and, to use her own words,
" such a happy creature, full of his jokes." He was
engaged as second engineer at £4 10s. and board.
" After his ship was loaded ' he was a changed man,' he
' got his tea without saying a word,' and then ' sat looking
into the fire in a deep study like.' I asked him what ailed
him, and he said, more to himself than me, ' She is such a
beast!' I thought he meant the men's place was dirty, as
he had complained before that there was nowhere for the
men to wash. He liked to be clean, my husband, and
always had a good wash when he came home from the
workshop, when he worked ashore. So I said, ' Will you
let me come aboard to clean it for ye?' and he said, still
looking at the fire, ' It isn't that.' Well, he hadn't signed,
only agreed, so I said, ' Don't sign, Jim;' and he said he
wouldn't, and went and told the engineer he shouldn't go.
The engineer ' spoke so kindly to him,' and offered him
10s. a month more. He'd had no work for a long time,
and the money was tempting," she said, " so he signed.
When he told me, I said, ' Oh! Jim, you won't go, will
you?' He said, ' Why, hinnie, hinnie, they'll put me in
gaol if I don't.' I said, ' Never mind, ye can come home
after that.' ' But,' said he, ' they'll call me a coward, and
ye wouldn't like to hear me called that.'"

The poor woman was crying very bitterly, so I said
gently, " I hope you won't think I am asking all these
questions from idle curiosity;" and I shall never forget her
quick disclaimer, for she saw that I was troubled with her—
" Oh no, sir, I am glad to answer you; for so many homes
might be spared being made desolate if it was only looked
into."

I ascertained that she is now "getting a bit winning for a livelihood," as my informant phrased it (of course I was not so rude as to ask her that), by sewing for a ready-made clothes shopkeeper. She was in a small garret, with a sloping roof, and the most modest fireplace I ever saw—just three bits of iron laid from side to side of an opening in the brickwork, and two more up the front; no chimney-piece, or jambs, or stone across the top, but just the bricks laid nearer and nearer until the courses united. So I don't fancy she could be earning much. But with the very least money value in the place, it was as beautifully clean as I ever saw a room in my life.

I saw also Mrs. W——ks, of 78, B——d Street, who had lost her son, Henry W——ks, aged twenty-two. She too cried bitterly as she spoke with *such* love and pride of her son, and of the grief of his father, who was sixty years of age. Her son was taken on as stoker, and worked in the ship some days before she was ready for sea. He didn't want to go then, when he saw how she was loaded; but they refused to pay him the money he had earned unless he went; and he too was lost with all the others.

Just one more specimen of the good, true, and brave men we sacrifice by our most cruel and manslaughtering neglect, and then I will go on to the next part of my subject.

This time I went to 17, D——h Street, and called upon old J——n P——r, and after apologising for intruding upon his grief, I asked him if he had any objection to telling me whether his son had had any misgivings about the ship before he went. He said, "Yes. I went to see the ship myself, and I was horrified to see the way she was loaded. She looked like a floating wreck; and I tried all I could to persuade him not to go; but he'd been doing nothing for a long time, and he didn't like being a burthen on me. 'He'd a fine 'sperrit,' sir, had my son," said the poor old man.

Here a young woman I had not observed (she was in a corner, with her face to the wall) broke out into loud sobs, and said, "He was the best of us all, sir—the best in the whole family.   He was as fair as a flower, and vah-y canny-looking."

Oh! my God! my God! what can I say, what can I write, to make the people take thought on this terrible wrong?

I tell you, you who read these lines, if you are a man, you deserve to perish suddenly, lacking sympathy and succour in your hour of utmost need, and leaving your nearest and dearest only the cold charity of the world to depend upon—for this is how sailors die—if you don't help. If you are a wife, you deserve that your husband should be taken from you without warning, and that to the anguish of bereavement should be added the material miseries of hunger and destitution—for this is how sailors' wives suffer —if you do not help.   If you are a father, descending it may be into the vale of years, with sons strong and brave, the pride and support of your age, you deserve that they should suddenly perish with no hand to help them, leaving your remaining years uncheered by one filial greeting—for so the fathers of sailors are bereaved—if you do not help. If you are a mother, you deserve that your son should be taken from you in the pride of his young manhood, if you don't help to stop this homicidal, this manslaughtering, this widow-and-orphan manufacturing system.

Fellow Christians, have you nothing to say to this?   Do you think that there are no religious sailors—no followers of our common Lord and Saviour amongst them?   Oh, but you are greatly mistaken.   There is more true religion amongst miners and sailors than you are aware.

Don't you recollect the miner at the Hartley accident who slid down the guide-rods, knowing he could not get up again for days it might be, that he might pray with and for his companions who were below the broken engine-beam, and who could never more see the light?

Do you forget the loving husband who in that horrible pit, face to face with death, scratched with his knife on a breakfast can a message of love to his wife Sarah?

I have been aboard a ship when the sailors were holding a service in the forecastle, a single lamp swinging from the deck beam, and wild rough weather without, making you hold on to a pillar to stand, and this was the order of it. They commenced by singing Toplady's beautiful hymn, which solaced poor Prince Albert when he lay on his all-too-early death-bed—

> " Rock of ages, cleft for me,
> Let me hide myself in thee ;
> Let the water and the blood
> From thy wounded side which flowed,
> Be of sin the double cure,
> Save from wrath and make me pure."

Then followed the reading of a chapter and prayer. Then this hymn—

> " Abide with me, fast falls the eventide,
> The darkness thickens ; Lord, with me abide,
> When other helpers fail and comforts flee,
> Help of the helpless, oh, abide with me."

Then the big, bluff captain, with the Union Jack for cover, and a hogshead on end for a reading-desk, gave a short, earnest sermon from—" Behold, I stand at the door, and knock : if any man hear my voice, and open unto me, I will come in to him and make my abode with him ;" and then they concluded with the hymn—

> " One there is, above all others,
> Well deserves the name of friend,"

and I well remember their singing the verse—

> "Which of all our friends, to save us,
> Could or would have shed his blood ? "

and wondering how it was that these brave men were so entirely friendless—how it was that they alone of British subjects should have been abandoned to the tender mercies of unchecked irresponsibility—of competition run mad.

Have you no word to say when you are shown, on evidence you *cannot* doubt, that your fellow Christians are sent down to death, and their wives made widows, their children fatherless, when you could prevent it by the simple expression of your will ? Oh ! shame, shame ! how will you answer to the Master for it, when you and they stand at length before Him ?

Fellow Loyalists,—You who are thankful for the inesti-
mable blessings of a settled Government, and who are unwilling that this glorious England of ours should incur the
tremendous loss of dignity which would ensue from having
the highest person in the nation subjected to all the abuse
which malignity and falsehood can allege or invent, every
four years, and who are, besides being loyal, deeply attached
to our good Queen : I call upon you to help, for I feel absolutely sure she would, if she should ever hear how the matter
stands. You cannot forget how she telegraphed, day after
day, while there was any hope of rescuing the poor men who
were interred alive in the Hartley Colliery.

Working men, is it nothing to you that your fellow-work-
men, fathers of families, men to whom life is as dear as it is
to yourselves, men who have committed no fault, should
thus shamefully be neglected?—should thus be drowned by
the dozen and the score to make a few bad men richer?—
and that their needless deaths should not elicit an inquiry
into the cause of it? I hate to appeal to class feelings or
prejudices, but class jealousy can only be allayed by justice,
·not by ignoring murderous wrong ; and I ask, seriously and
sadly, can any one doubt, but that if these brave men had
been pigs or sheep, the Legislature had long since been
compelled by powerful advocates to stop such losses? Pigs
and sheep are property, and property is well represented in
Parliament ; but these—why, they are only our poor brothers,
and no one speaks for them.

I do not wish to represent Parliament as indifferent to
the interests of working men. On the contrary, it is
impossible to contemplate the fiscal legislation of the past
twenty years without gratefully acknowledging on their
behalf its unselfish, nay, more, its self-denying character ;
but, when no pressing demand is made for the remedy of
social wrong, its removal is postponed to those matters which
are pressed. Parliament will act readily enough if people out
of doors make it a prominent question; and, so thoroughly am
I satisfied on this point, that I begin to doubt whether I was
right in trying to get into Parliament with the object of

getting this done. It seems to me at least doubtful whether I should not have done better to have endeavoured to rouse people out of doors to the urgency of the matter. At any rate, on this I have decided, that if, during the coming Session, I again fail to obtain at least a Royal Commission to inquire into the subject, I will restore to my constituents the high trust they confided to me, and will then, as God may help me, and with such fellow-workers as I may find, go from town to town, and tell the story of the sailors' wrongs. For, if the working men of Sheffield, Leeds, Birmingham, and Manchester only demand justice for these poor men, the thing is done. The working men of Derby have done their part, for when, moved by the sailors' wrongs, I asked them to send me to Parliament to seek for justice, they sent me by over 2,000 majority.

Gentlemen of the Press,—Your great power and influence have always been exercised on behalf of the oppressed. Nor has their inability to even thank you stayed the generous exercise of your power, else one might despair of these men, for they are politically perfectly helpless; they can neither threaten a ministry nor offer a contingent to the opposition; they are not even your supporters as readers, for, divided into small groups of a dozen or a score, they spend their lives for the most part far away at sea, and know not, even if they were able to invoke it, how great is the help you can give them. This will not render you less willing to help them, their case understood, and I have diligently done my poor best to gather for you the materials for forming a judgment on it.

Help them then, I pray you, and you too shall be helped by the recollection of your brotherly aid when that hour comes when you will need the help of Him that sticketh closer than a brother. Consider how not only are the sailors' lives sacrificed, not only are many, very many of their wives made widows, but what a clouded life all their wives lead from well-grounded and constant apprehension, which, deeply depressing at all times, knows no other variation than the quick agony into which those apprehensions are aroused whenever the wind rises even to a moderate gale.

Whoever you are who read this, help the poor sailors, for the love of God. If you are a man of influence, call a meeting and confer on this Appeal; if you are not, and will write to me, I will try to show you how to help.

If you refuse—but this I cannot think—but if you refuse or neglect to use your influence, before another year has run its course at least five hundred—five hundred men!—now in life, will strew the bottom of the sea with their dead, unburied, unresting bodies, and desolation and woe will have entered many and many a now happy home; but if you do render your help, we can secure such life-preserving activity in precautionary measures that the sailor will have no fear; and then the storms of winter may come, but with good tight ships under them, and sound gear to their hands, their own strong arms and stout hearts can do the rest, and as, after a night of storm and tempest, which but for your fraternal care would have overwhelmed them in death and sent bereavement and anguish into their humble homes, they reach their desired haven, weary and worn it may be, but still safe—chilled to the marrow, but still alive—the blessings of those who are ready to perish shall be yours: nor shall there be lacking to you those richer blessings promised by the Great Father of us all, to those who visit the widow and fatherless, for that to the high and the noble and the sacred duty of visiting them in their affliction, you have preferred the higher, the nobler, and the yet more sacred duty of saving women and children from so sad a fate.

SAMUEL PLIMSOLL.

III, VICTORIA STREET, LONDON, S.W.
March, 1873.

THE END.

PRINTED BY VIRTUE AND CO., CITY ROAD, LONDON.

Lightning Source UK Ltd.
Milton Keynes UK
UKOW06n1448181115

262996UK00011B/113/P